BACK COVER

Letters to the Editor: From the Trenches of Democracy Volume 5 is a unique account of the author's 20-year labor at one of the purest forms of free speech; writing letters to the editor regarding his concerns about the present and our future.

The author shares his personal history, which led to his success in having letters published in his local and regional newspapers, national newspapers and newsmagazines.

The book contains helpful tips on writing letters and 154 of the author's published letters commenting on major national, state and local news events and issues over the past 2 years, with emphasis on the abuse of power by President Obama and the 2014 mid-term elections. Together with Volumes 1, 2, 3 and 4 of his work covering the previous 18 years, the author has 671 published letters. Volume 3 contains the author's unpublished letters (2007-2011). Volumes 4 and 5 include unpublished letters.

As the author says, "I cannot leave my country, my state, my community and my family with anything less."

(AUTHOR PHOTO) Dan Jeffs is the founder of the Direct Democracy Center. He is retired from a 41-year career in the criminal justice system, and he holds a law degree and a teaching credential. Jeffs is the author of *America's Crisis: The Direct Democracy and Direct Education Solution* (featured on C-Span Book TV).

LETTERS
TO THE EDITOR

From the Trenches of Democracy

Volume 5

President Obama vs. America - Round 7:

2014 mid-term elections

By

DANIEL B. JEFFS

To Scott,
with best regards,

[signature]

[signature]

March 28, 2015

ISBN: 1507709226
ISBN 13: 9781507709221

DEDICATION

To my fellow letter writers

Latest published letters and commentary by Daniel B. Jeffs

VV Daily Press
March 6, 2015

President and leftist Dems

ObamaCare, ObamaFinance, ObamaEnergy, and now the ObamaNet are making it painfully clear that President Obama's ObamAmerica and leftist Democrats – including Hollywood -- are the party of tyranny against the best interests of the American people with destructive regulations, punishing taxation and unsustainable national debt.

Worse, President Obama's legacy is on reckless course to disarm the United States in the face of dictator Putin's Russian aggression, a rapidly expanding Islamic terrorist movement – and feigned negotiations with Iran's nuclear weapons state, regardless of Israeli Prime Minister Netanyahu's real warnings and self-defense – all of which threaten to annihilate Israel, America and the West.

Clearly, it's bad enough that the counter-culture revolutionists have turned our country into a superficial society of social injustice, political chaos, selfish interests, economic instability, steeped in uncertainty, and extremes. Indeed, the Boomer generation is now well on the way to overwhelming Medicare after developing a nation of fools by indoctrination, distractions, deceptions, lies, the insidious intended consequences of failed good intentions, and the loss of freedoms. That is what a socialist takeover is all about.

Alas, the next two years will be our nation's reckoning with the enemy within the 7th round of President Obama and his minions vs. America, with only the Republican Party and the informed people standing in the way of an 8th round knockout. Surely, Mr. Obama's White House is a "House of Cards" stain on the presidency. Attention: Republican Congress, governors and presidential nominee! Strong language and action is what is needed -- for our survival and restoration. The washed-out Washington way simply won't cut it!

The Washington Times
March 4, 2015

Netanyahu right on Iran

House Speaker Boehner was wise to have Israeli Prime Minister Benjamin Netanyahu speak to Congress to address the truth about Iran's evil designs to rule the Middle East. Prime Minister Netanyahu displayed candid courage in the face of being snubbed by President Obama and his Democrat minions, while his Secretary of State, John Kerry was busy capitulating to Iran's one-side negotiations.

Indeed, President Obama's passive legacy is on reckless course to disarm the United States in the face of dictator Vladimir Putin's aggression, a rapidly expanding Islamic terrorist movement and hapless negotiations with Iran (regardless of Prime Minister Netanyahu's warnings) all of which threaten to annihilate Israel, America and the West.

Surely, Mr. Netanyahu is well known as a fearless defender of his homeland. And certainly, Israel will know if and when it's time to strike Iran to prevent their nuclear weapons capability, even though Mr. Obama has wrongly warned them against unilateral action.

Iran is a clear and present danger to Israel and our national security. The president and Congress must take decisive action or the consequences will be ours. Anything less is unacceptable. Alas, though unthinkable, there is nothing to prevent Russia and/or North Korea from providing Iran with nuclear weapons.

VV Daily Press
March 1, 2015

President Obama's poison pens

President Obama's executive order and administration arrogance continues with a Keystone Pipeline veto against the economy, and his FCC move under the guise of Net Neutrality to control the Internet and squelch free speech.

Indeed, it's bad enough that Mr. Obama's poison executive order pen – and now his poison veto pen -- have been working overtime against our energy and our economy. But when he moves to control our freedom of communications over the internet, coupled with his undue influence over the news media, our liberty is threatened.

Worse, it is well known and understood that this president has surrendered our national security to Islamic terrorism, Russian aggression and the inevitability of a nuclear weaponized Iran. And, coupled with his reckless reductions of our military and nuclear strength, the real clear and present danger to America has become President Obama and his minions.

Adding insult to injury, California's government abuse of power and environmental extremists exacerbates the plight of the people with land-grabs, over-regulation, punishing taxation, dangerous water shortages, costly illegal immigrant sanctuary, and the escalation of crime.

Fortunately, we still have the right to voter initiative, referendum and recall, which will extend the July deadline and give us the chance to keep our plastic grocery bags with a win in the November 2016 election.

VV Daily Press
February 25, 2015

Re: Al Vogler - Valley Voices
Daily Press Opinion, Feb 22, 2015

Water crisis runs deep

Al Vogler's concerns are shared by all Southern California property owners who paid for and maintain the California Water Project, which was constructed to provide Sacramento Delta Northern California water resources to millions of water users in Southern California – particularly, after suffering years of drought conditions.

However, even after the recent rains, the man-made drought continues because of the Natural Resources Defense Council extremists and a federal judge cutting water supplies nearly in half to protect the tiny Delta Smelt fish at the expense of human health and welfare.

Of course this has resulted in the constant and unnecessary dumping millions of acre-feet of fresh water into the sea, which should have been going to quench the thirst of farms and water users in Central and Southern California.

As a 2007/2008 county grand jury member, my committee investigated county water resources from several California Water Project contractors among those who service water contracts from the Project throughout Southern California.

As a result of my investigation, I was clearly outraged by the fact that the federal judge and other state water authorities have seriously and continuously violated the Constitution's prohibition of government interference with private contracts.

Indeed, it should be strongly suggested that the California Water Project Contractors Association and/or property owner users -- of which I am one – file state and federal lawsuits to restore all Project water resources cut off by the federal court at the behest of extremist groups and supported by state and federal officials. The Constitution certainly demands it.

The Washington Times
February 25, 2015

Oscars miss the mark again

The 2015 Academy Awards was simply the final round of Hollywood celebrating itself again – and again and again. Alas, with few exceptions, the film and entertainment industry continues to decline into little more than sex, violence, shallow stories, lack of imagination and original thought reduced to narcissism resembling "Fifty Shades of Grey."

As for the exceptions, mostly-true stories such as "Selma," "The Theory of Everything," "The imitation Game," "Foxcatcher," "American Sniper," "Still Alice," "Boyhood," and "Whiplash" rounded out the exceptions. However, "Birdman or (The unexpected Virtue of Ignorance)" overshadowed them all with the darkness of mass neurosis that consumes the hopelessly self-involved. "Best Picture" and "Best Director"? Hardly.

Certainly, the only clarity coming from the Oscars dog-and-pony costume show was the host with least, Neil Patrick Harris, those promoting liberal social and political issues and the whiners. Snubbing the genuine talent and integrity of the real best director, Clint Eastwood, epitomizes the intolerance and the ongoing lack of morality that is Hollywood.

However the name fits. Holly is supposed to be a symbol of joy – yet its leaves are extremely prickly, guarding a soul of wood. Society needs a do-over.

VV Daily Press
February 23, 2015

Community organizing not the answer
Contrary to President Obama's naïve experience with community organizing, his feckless global summit focusing on the empowerment of local communities to counter the violent extremism of ISIS, al-Qaeda and other Islamic terrorists with social justice, strong leadership, families, opportunity, education, economic improvement and jobs is simply ludicrous.

Certainly, decades of the failed war on poverty and community organizing resulted in the unresolved liberal government's proliferation of disorganized, disoriented, irresponsible welfare neighborhoods, miseducation, single mothers, absent fathers, drugs, gangs, violent crime and perpetual anger in vulnerable American communities, which are living proof that it doesn't work.

Alas, it's become painfully clear that President Obama has abdicated his role as the free world leader against radical Islamic terrorism by allowing the not holy, but unholy war by evil savages against the good world to proliferate. Indeed, the unintended consequence of the failures of good intentions is not an option against terrorists bent on world domination. It's intentional insanity.

San Diego Union-Tribune
February 22, 2015

Unions hurt economy and themselves
The selfish interests of striking dockworker union bosses at California and West Coast ports are simply being self-destructive for their union members, and damaging to thousands of other workers, local and state businesses, their employees, and the overall California and U.S. economy.

That's simply insane in these perilous economic times. Alas, that seems to be the long-term negative destiny caused by California's intrusive liberal government's social, political, and economic disservice to the people of the state and the nation.

(original letter)

Unions are damaging themselves and the California economy
The selfish interests of striking dockworker union bosses at California and West Coast ports are simply being self-destructive for their union members, and damaging to thousands of other workers, local and state businesses, their employees, and the overall California and U.S. economy.

That's simply insane in these perilous economic times. Alas, that seems to be the long-term negative destiny caused by California's intrusive liberal government's social, political, and economic disservice to the people of the state and the nation.

Indeed, it's far past time to get out of reckless and costly union traps and get in to economic freedom and the right to work.

Riverside Press Enterprise
February 21, 2015
(lead letter)

Allowing ISIS to flourish

President Obama has abdicated his role as the leader of the free world. He has allowed an unholy war by evil savages against the good world to proliferate.

Contrary to what a State department spokeswoman recently said, Islamic State atrocities simply cannot be countered by the ludicrous suggestion of getting them jobs.

Indeed, the unintended consequence of the failures of good intentions is not an option against terrorists. It's intentional insanity.

VV Daily Press
February 19, 2015

ISIS atrocities a holy war?

It's become painfully clear that President Obama has abdicated his role as the free world leader against radical Islamic terrorism by allowing the, not holy, but unholy war by evil savages against the good world to proliferate. Contrary to what a State department spokeswoman recently said, ISIS atrocities simply cannot be countered by the ludicrous suggestion of getting them jobs. Indeed, the unintended consequence of the failures of good intentions is not an option against terrorists. It's intentional insanity.

VV Daily Press
February 11, 2015

Senator Feinstein's monuments

Senator Dianne Feinstein is at it again by introducing legislation that would increase federal control over 1.6 million acres of our Mojave Desert.

It was bad enough that Feinstein picked up former senator Cranston's efforts against the desert, but she apparently won't be satisfied until she established absolute federal power over our lands.

Worse, President Obama is bound and determined to do the same thing throughout the country, particularly seizing power over our natural resources such as coal, oil and all mining.

Indeed, abuse of power has become a standard practice for Mr. Obama in his efforts to fundamentally transform America to fit his ideology, regardless of how it affects our economy and our freedoms.

A citizen's word of advice to President Obama, Senator Feinstein and intrusive government, including California's government: Keep your noses out of our business, our lives and our liberty. And keep in mind what "local control" means to the states and the people.

Monuments are only for people who earn it.

NEWSMAX Magazine
February issue 2015

Race tensions rise
After decades of progress, race relations are obviously worse since President Obama was elected and became an imperial president ("Success wins over black victimhood," December 2014).

Race relations will certainly deteriorate even further as the protests continue and grow throughout the country, invading streets, highways and freeways, blocking traffic and endangering the public. President Obama should step-up to improve race relations as a major part of his legacy. If not, the insanity goes on, unabated.

Lest we forget, the police are our first line of defense in neighborhoods, communities, and cities against criminals and terrorists.

(original letter)

Race relations in America
After decades of progress, race relations are obviously worse since President Obama was elected and became an imperial president, to the extent of giving African-Americans an arrogant superiority

complex and/or being treated as sacred cows in the Obama era. Indeed, Hollywood and advertisers have responded by over-representing blacks in films, television and commercials.

Worse, racial protests, demonstrations, rioting, arson and looting have been exacerbated by President Obama, his aggressively radical race counselor, Al Sharpton, indoctrinated college students and the complicit news media -- touched off by the Travon Martin case -- then magnified by the Michael Brown and Eric Garner death cases at the hands of police -- who were not indicted by local grand juries.

Race relations will certainly deteriorate even further as the protests continue and grow throughout the country, invading streets, highways and freeways, blocking traffic and endangering the public – even blocking Christmas shoppers in stores and malls. President Obama should step-up to improve race relations as a major part of his legacy. If not, the insanity goes on, unabated......

Lest we forget, the police are our first line of defense in neighborhoods, communities and cities against criminals and terrorists.

Commentary
By Daniel B. Jeffs

VV Daily Press
Commentary
February 24, 2015

Hollywood celebrating itself, again....

The 2015 Academy Awards was simply the final round of Hollywood celebrating itself again, and again, and again.... Alas, with few exceptions, the film and entertainment industry continues to decline into little more than sex, violence, shallow stories, lack of imagination and original thought reduced to fifty shades of grey narcissism.

As for the exceptions, mostly-true stories such as "Selma," "The Theory of Everything," "The imitation Game," "Foxcatcher" and "American Sniper" – and "Still Alice," "Boyhood," plus "Whiplash" – rounded out the exceptions. However, "Birdman or (The unexpected Virtue of Ignorance)" over-shadowed them all with the darkness of mass neurosis that consumes the hopelessly self-involved. Best Picture and Best Director? Hardly.

Certainly, the only clarity coming from the Oscars dog and pony costume show was the host with least, those promoting liberal social and political issues, and the whiners. Snubbing the genuine talent and integrity of the real best director, Clint Eastwood, is the intolerance and the ongoing lack of morality that is Hollywood.

However the name fits. Holly is supposed to be a symbol of joy – yet it's leaves are extremely prickly, guarding a soul of wood. Society needs a do-over.

Daniel B. Jeffs

Commentary
by Daniel B. Jeffs
February 3, 2015

President Obama vs. America
(Round 7 starts with a $4 trillion budget)
In the deadly hostile environment of ISIS, al-Qaeda and Taliban terrorists, it has become painfully clear that President Obama is covering his arrogant ineptness and refusal to deal with the imminent dangers to our national security by insulting the intelligence of the American people.

Indeed, since when did Taliban terrorists -- controlling Afghanistan and joining with Osama bin-Laden's al-Qaeda to plot and carry out the 9/11 attacks on America -- become *insurgents*?

The answer is simple: Since the president traded 5 top level Taliban terrorists for Army Sgt. Bowe Bergdahl, an American deserter and traitor who collaborated with the Taliban for 5 years, costing the lives of 5 of our troops searching for him. Since President Obama surrendered Iraq, Syria, Afghanistan and Middle East to Iran and the radical Islamic Jihad against all non-conforming Muslims, Israel, America and the West.

Surely, Mr. Obama's Taliban prisoner exchange intentions were to appease the Taliban – followed by closing Guantanamo and giving it back to Cuba -- suppress Bergdahl's military prosecution and quietly slip him out of the military with a dishonorable discharge – not to mention ignoring the ongoing Taliban terrorist takeover of nuclear Pakistan, recently costing the lives of 132 school children.

President Obama is the antithesis of a responsible U.S. President and Commander-in-Chief, and he is betraying the American people with his dangerous ineptness, distractions, deceptions, lies, abuse of power machinations and parsing official language – too numerous to include here -- in the blind pursuit of his un-American agenda

Unfortunately, impeachment is not an option for the first black president. Hopefully, with an $18 trillion national debt, and coming out with a $4 trillion budget in Round 7, America can survive the sucker-punches of Mr. Obama's last two years in office. And hopefully, wised-up voters, a reformed media and a Republican president and Congress can undo what Obama/Democrats have wrought upon our society and lead us out of the liberal wilderness to the light of freedom and recovery.

President Obama is waging war against coal, oil and much more

President Obama and his liberal Democrat culture have been waging war against America since his 2008 election. Clearly, the president's latest attack against oil by designating 1.5 million oil-rich acres in Alaska a wilderness area, and refusal to approve the Keystone Pipeline -- added to his EPA's crushing blows against the coal industry -- is painful proof of his campaign promise that our electric bills would necessarily "skyrocket," in favor of costly and unreliable renewable energy.

Indeed, we now know that when then Senator Obama boldly stated that he was going to fundamentally transform America -- by undermining our security and freedoms with extreme social, political and economic divisions -- he meant it.

Certainly, President Obama and his Democrat Congress undermined our economic freedoms with his Unaffordable Careless Act, and the Dodd Frank finance legislation. Worse, Mr. Obama's foreign policy and feckless war against terrorism has put our nation at extreme risk, particularly by playing into the feigned negotiating hands of the world's largest state sponsor of terrorism, Iran while they develop nuclear weapons and expand their influence throughout the Middle East – with little or no resistance.

Surely, President Obama blatantly lied in his 2015 State of the Union speech when he said that he had no more campaigns to run, when in fact he has never stopped campaigning, and won't stop during his last two years in office. The question is, how much more damage will he inflict upon us? Fortunately, Congress is now controlled by Republicans, albeit subject to Mr. Obama's veto. Hopefully, the presidency will go to a Republican in 2016 instead of incompetent Hillary Clinton – a poor choice for the first woman president – as it sadly was for the first black president.

Alas, America is steeped in uncertainty from being assaulted by big government, abuse of power, regulations taxation and debt – and battered by the failures of good intentions. Hopefully, the Republican Party will nominate Wisconsin Governor Scott Walker, with an articulate running-mate such as Sen. Rubio or Gov. Huckabee. Governor Walker is an honest man with high integrity, state executive experience, and he will be strong for our society, our economy and our national security.

Clearly, our freedoms, our future, our security and democracy are in the hands of our fellow voters – a voter nation of fools -- until we took control of the House in 2010, slipped back to President Obama in 2012 – then took control of the Senate in 2014. We will need someone like Governor Walker in 2016, to pick up the pieces of our unique republic, recover and move on to true liberty real democracy and prosperity.

Daniel B. Jeffs

Acknowledgements

I wish to thank and acknowledge all of the newspapers and news-magazines that published my letters to the editor.

In terms of television news, I would like to extend my appreciation to *NewsCorp* and the *Fox News Channel* for providing fair and balanced truth in reporting the news, in stark contrast to what is disturbingly disseminated by the biased news cartel of *ABC, CBS, NBC, CNN* and most major print news media. Fortunately, print media such as the *Wall Street Journal, New York Post,* the *Washington Times, Washington Examiner* and *Freedom Communications* print media practice responsible journalism.

And I must echo the sentiment, "Thank you *C-Span*" for their neutral, uncut coverage of politics, government, social and economic policy without editorials. An additional thank you goes to *C-Span* for providing unparalleled public access to telephone and email democracy. Real democracy is being practiced at *C-Span*.

Of course, there is a great appreciation to information and communications technology industry, and the purveyors of the Internet for dramatically expanding the voice of the people, democracy, freedom of expression and the resources for limitless information.

However, I am deeply concerned about the dark side of the rapidly advancing social media era, and much worse, the ominous side of cyber crime and terrorism that affects our politics, economics, society and national security.

CONTENTS

AND INDEX TO PUBLISHED LETTERS

FOREWORD

We have it in our power to begin the world over again.

— Thomas Paine
Common Sense

The only thing necessary for evil to exist is for good people to
remain silent.

— Edmund Burke
(paraphrased)

America is steeped in uncertainty. Our society has been
relentlessly assaulted by selfish interests and battered by the
failures of good intentions. The time to save our democracy is
now.

— Daniel B. Jeffs
America's Crisis

Our nation has been unduly influenced by a superficial society of socialist aggression, political chaos, selfish interests and extremes. We must hold on to our liberty, and keep a tight grip on our freedom.

The shame of good deeds is they are not appreciated for generations. The tragedy of bad deeds is they are not resisted until it's too late.

— Daniel B. Jeffs
Letters to the Editor

INTRODUCTION

It has been profoundly said, and how true it is, that the only thing necessary for evil to exist is for good people to remain silent. — Edmund Burke (paraphrased)

Sometime during most people's lives they have either written or had the urge to write a letter to the editor of their newspaper. The event is usually brought on by something they perceive as good or bad that happened in their community, their state or the nation. People are often stimulated by strong feelings about something they have personally experienced, seen on television or read in the newspaper.

Unfortunately, most people's letters don't get published. The main reason is that newspapers simply receive too many letters to publish them all. Other reasons range from rambling, lengthy letters, to angry letters that are too inflammatory, or letters that simply don't make sense.

Most editors prefer concise letters, limited to between 150 and 300 words, which they can tie-in or "tag" to "hot-button" issues covered by their newspapers.

Over twenty years ago I began to write letters about issues I felt strongly about. I achieved some success with letters published in my local and regional newspapers. As I learned the language and the types of comments on issues that editors were looking for, my letters improved. Then I began submitting letters to national newspapers and newsmagazines, many of which were published. Letters from others with differing views on a particular issue have been included where possible.

This book contains helpful tips on writing letters and the 154 of the author's published letters commenting on major national, state and local news events and issues over the past 2 years, with emphasis on the abuse of power by President Obama and the 2014 mid-term elections. Together with Volumes 1, 2, 3 and 4 of his work covering the previous 18 years, the author has 671 published letters. Volume 3 contains the author's unpublished letters (2007-2011). Volumes 4 and 5 include unpublished letters.

One objective of this book is to help you write letters to the editor that will have a better chance at being published. In addition to suggestions for writing letters to the editor, I have included a few tips on writing other effective letters. After all, most of us would like to be heard from down here in the trenches of democracy and we need all the help we can get.

Regardless of your views, as you read through the book, it should assist you in creating issues, arguing issues and to develop your own commentary and letter-writing style. Learn the media's language, be concise, keep writing and your voice will be heard.

We must never underestimate the power of our words. Unless we break your silence, support what we believe in and speak out against tyranny and injustice, we cannot expect to hold on to our liberty.

The September 11, 2001 attack on America and the war against terrorism abruptly changed our lives. Terrorist attacks against us around the world continue, and we remain under the threat of another terrorist attack on our homeland -- possibly a nuclear attack.

The 2008 economic collapse, the election of Barack Obama as president, and the Democrat-controlled Congress seriously diminished our individual liberties and freedoms, and reduced our national security. Now, more than ever, we must be aware of what is going on in our society, our government and around the world. We should educate ourselves, ask questions and demand answers. Writing letters to the editor is an accessible way to do it, and one of the most valuable tools of free speech.

It's time for the silent majority of middle-America to speak out, as is being done with the spontaneous Tea Party movement reacting to the over-reaching expansion, regulation, taxation and control by government. Fortunately, the Tea Party movement resulted in Republicans taking control of the House of Representative, and gaining seats in the Senate in 2010.

Unfortunately, President Obama was re-elected, Democrats gained more seats in the Senate, and the Republican House is the only thing keeping us from being consumed by forces beyond our control and losing our democracy. Fortunately, Republicans gained control of the Senate in 2014, and their seats in the House. President Obama is now at war against the Republican Congress and our economy, but neglecting our national security and failing in the war against terrorism.

Hopefully, Republicans will win the presidency in 2016 and restore our democracy.

Meanwhile, the expansion of the Internet, communications technology, and new media has extended a wealth of information and potential power to all the people. We must use and protect it or lose it to government control and/or cyber attacks from our enemies.

I have spoken out many times on social, political and economic issues and I will continue to do so as long as I am able. I simply cannot leave my family, my community, my state and my country with anything less...

TRIBUTE TO MY SON

Dick Armey's Freedom Works organization conducted a 2009 "I am and Entrepreneur" essay contest in which my submission was one of the winners.

Following is my submission:
http://www.freedomworks.org/content/my-son-is-an-entrepreneur

My son is an Entrepreneur
By Daniel B. Jeffs
Apple Valley, CA
March 7, 2009

My son, John T. Jeffs (nick name: "Jay") is a 42-year-old self-made entrepreneur and innovator. And, of course, I couldn't be prouder of him. Jay is a great man, married with a daughter. He is too modest and humble to tell his own unique story, so I will.

Before I begin, It should be noted that against all odds, Jay built his small business from nothing, in Apple Valley, CA, the town where he lives, employing local people and providing the important products of security mail handling equipment. Of course, his constant challenge has been surviving the unyielding anti-business environment of extreme taxation and regulations by California government. A remarkable accomplishment.

Children are often asked, "What do you want to be when you grow up?" While Jay was excavating a project in the dirt yard with his Tonka trucks, I asked him the question. He replied, "I'm gonna be a workin' man." And that's what he became. While growing up he wanted to work with me around the house and yard, making improvements and working on the car. He loved to work with tools and to make things. In junior high school woodshop, he made an amazing laminated cutting board for his mother from various hardwoods. She still uses it today.

Jay's work ethic was established early. He helped the family when times were tough, skipped high school sports so he could work after school and contribute his paycheck, and he never complained. His first job was working at a local pizza parlor, then for a new Carl's Jr. in town, where he worked his way up to assistant manager. Then we worked for the Old Quaker Paint Company, saved his money, and bought into a quick-lube business. Soon after, he joined a credit union and established his first credit with a small loan.

But Jay wasn't satisfied with working for others. He wanted to start his own business and be an entrepreneur. While still working at the paint company and quick lube, he decided to do something no one else was doing. Sell, install and repair curbside mailboxes for people. It was 1987, and the U.S. Postal Service was changing to curbside service from mail trucks instead of door to door mail service. The curbside mailbox was the last thing new homeowners installed, which were not included when new homes were built. It was a chore because people had to buy a mailbox, post and house numbers, along with a posthole digger if they didn't have one. Plus, most curbside mailboxes were rural-style, not secure and easily damaged by vandals with bats, or broken by being struck by vehicles.

Jay placed an ad describing his new service in the local newspaper. The basic service was for a box, post and numbers installed for $30.00. At first the response was slow, but when people responded, word-of-mouth increased the business. Jay had a pick-up truck, and he used my hand tools, power tools and posthole digger to do the work. He purchased mailboxes from a distributor and offered several styles and models. Then when tracts of homes were being built in the area, he obtained a contract to install mailboxes, which led to additional contracts. It was less expensive for builders to subcontract with Jay than to use their own carpenters.

It wasn't long before Jay expanded to sales and installations of commercial and residential multiple mailbox units, which he purchased from a dealer in the Los Angeles area. The dealer was also a commercial mail handling equipment contractor who asked Jay to do installations for them because they lost their installer. Jay agreed and expanded his experience to installing equipment in mailrooms, office and apartment buildings, along with mail chutes, bank chutes and laundry chutes in high rise buildings. Subsequently, he obtained his own specialty contractor's license. And he received a timely $3,000 inheritance from a great uncle who sensed something special in Jay as an eager toddler.

While all this was going on, our home became a mailbox business. Jay used the garage for his shop, and the mailboxes were assembled in the house by my wife. He bought a larger truck, more power tools, built several sheds to store product and supplies, and the house was filled with assembled boxes. Then Jay took a bigger step and began bidding on and getting more commercial and larger jobs, including apartments and mobile home parks. It wasn't long before my wife and I had to run away from home. We sold the house to Jay, and bought another home nearby.

With all the experience Jay absorbed, and the fact that mail theft was becoming a significant problem, Jay invented and patented the highest quality security mailbox available and trademarked it as the Letter Locker. After being tested and approved by the Postmaster General, the examiner was so impressed by it that he bought one. Soon, Jay built a large shop behind the house and began manufacturing the Letter Locker. He contracted out the fabrication, welding and powder-coating, and my wife did his office work and helped assemble Letter Lockers along with Jay's first employee. It wasn't long before our new garage was converted to assemble more boxes.

Jay secured more and more dealers for the Letter Locker and continued to expand, including the development of a rear loading model and a Supreme model that could receive and store more mail and larger parcels and packages. Then came the big step. He formed Jayco Industries as a limited liability corporation, and purchased a light industrial building on 15 acres where he manufactured the entire Letter Locker, which became the core of his business. He also became the largest western regional distributor for Auth-Florence mail handling equipment.

The business continued to grow, and by the turn of the century Jay had 85 dealers, 15 employees, 20 various size trucks, state-of-the-art metal manufacturing machinery. He expanded with satellite offices in Las Vegas, San Diego and Denver, and purchased the 15 acres of land next to his plant. When the USPS upgraded mailbox standards, they established security mailbox standards, using the Letter Locker as a model.

Jay recently invented an even more secure locking device for mailboxes, "The Claw Lock," which is available as an upgrade option on Letter Lockers, particularly, the heavy-duty model. He has websites for Letter Lockers and Jayco Industries at:
http://www.letterlocker.com and http://www.jaycoindustries.com

Of course, since the economic downturn in the housing market, Jay's business has slowed significantly. He is holding on as best as he can, supported by slower, but steady sales of Letter Lockers, commercial equipment and custom security boxes. Jay is a great employer and boss. He is fair and honest with his employees, who have the utmost respect for him. And he helps them out personally whenever he can. Though he is trying to keep them all employed, he has had to cut back on their hours, and close the Denver office.

Jay became the ideal entrepreneurial success story and he did it on pure self-reliance and hard work. He enjoys an excellent reputation for service in all his business dealings, and with the U.S. Postal Service. Needless to say, we are extremely proud parents, knowing that our son, John T. Jeffs is a well-respected example for anyone to aspire to in our democratic free market society. Indeed, I know of no one, other than my wife and daughter, who work as hard or have as much character and integrity as my son, Jay. For that, my wife and I are very successful family entrepreneurs.

As a footnote, I should add that my wife still assembles Letter Locker flag/bolt kits for the business at our home. And my daughter worked with Jay for a time as his director of operations. I retired in 2006 after working in law enforcement and as an investigator in the criminal justice system for a total of 41 years. I have always done all I could as an American citizen to ensure our continued security, liberty and freedom.

* * * *

May 11, 2009

Dear Daniel,

Thank you for entering our "I Am an Entrepreneur" competition to help us celebrate the entrepreneur. Congratulations! You are one of our runners-up--great work. We'll be sending your prize in the mail within the next two weeks.

If you'll send along your mailing information to Clark Ruper I'd appreciate it.

If you're interested, we have posted an announcement and links to all the winners on FreedomWorks.org

Thanks again for helping us celebrate the entrepreneur,

Joseph Onorati
Staff Writer
FreedomWorks

ENLIGHTENING
EXPERIENCES

To better understand my writing, a summary of my background might be helpful:

The most enlightening and fulfilling experience of my life has been my wife, Wilma and our children. Wilma and I raised two boys and a girl through the 60's, 70's and into the 80's. I began my life career as a cop in 1960. Wilma was a full-time mother, except during tough financial times. We were high school sweethearts and celebrated our 55th anniversary on July 31, 2014. When asked about the success of our long marriage my answer is, ups and downs notwithstanding, the most important thing is to be best friends. And it always helps to have a good dog as a member of the family.

My better half is undoubtedly the best wife, mother and partner on the planet. She was deeply involved with our children throughout their school years. We witnessed the beginning of the end of education as we knew it. If she hadn't supplemented their education at home, our children would not be the well-rounded people they are today. It took our combined efforts to teach them about character, consideration, discipline, friendship, work ethic, the ways of life, and to guide them through the failing social and political environment closing-in around them, which is something far more difficult for parents to deal with today. It is even more difficult and frustrating for single parents.

I was a deputy sheriff with the Los Angeles County Sheriff's Department from 1960 to 1967. During the first half of the decade the crime we identify with today was minimal. I worked the streets and neighborhoods and there were no significant problems with drugs, drunk-driving, domestic violence, sex crimes, child abuse, or guns and violence among young people. The civil rights movement and riots notwithstanding, there was mutual respect between law enforcement and the general public.

That all began to change when I went to work for the San Bernardino County Sheriff's Department (1967-1980). The social, political and criminal law revolution took hold. Elements of the baby boomer generation rejected their parents – now known as the greatest generation – and the so-called establishment. They launched the drug culture, took over education and, eventually, government. The rest is history, since revised, and I have personally witnessed most of it.

During my 20-year career as a patrolman, detective, sergeant, academy instructor and community college instructor I communicated with and observed people of all ages and from nearly every walk of life. I related to people on the streets, in their homes, where they went to school, where they worked and where the found recreation.

My approach to law enforcement changed when I realized that I didn't have to win every fight. I found it much more productive talking common sense with people and being fair and understanding. I discovered that many people could be helped at that most vulnerable moment in their lives when they crossed paths with a cop. It could be either a negative, often devastating experience, or a helpful learning experience.

The easy way was to carry a ten-pound badge and intimidate people. I found it difficult to work with other cops who acted like that. But it wasn't unusual during that brief period that I call "cop adolescence" when a young officer turns from an insecure rookie into a first-stage veteran. It happens after about 2 years on the job and it happened to me.

It's almost like being that indestructible teenager who knows everything, that is, until the raging hormones settle down and you're blinded by the stark reality that you have to get through the rest of life on your own. Most of us come out of it. Some don't and they're stuck in virtual immaturity. Unfortunately, if that happens to cops, they can be extremely dangerous to society.

Though it was often frowned upon in "cop shops", I established a good reputation with both prosecutors and defense attorneys because I would not seek a criminal complaint against anyone unless the investigation was honest and complete, both from a prosecution standpoint and a defense point of view. In other words, rather than focusing with prosecution blinders, I would resist arresting or trying to convict a person unless I was convinced by a thorough investigation that the person was guilty.

Some of my extraordinary experiences in law enforcement included the emerging reasons behind the Los Angeles Watts Riots of 1965 and working joint jurisdiction with the military at the 29 Palms Marine Corps Base in California during the controversial Vietnam War. My overall enlightening experience was the nation's cultural and political revolution that would lead to my leaving law enforcement in 1980. By then the writing was engraved on the wall.

Thomas Paine was 39 when he took on the passionate cause of freedom from tyranny. Though I don't pretend to be a Thomas Paine, I too was 39 when a similar burning desire first surfaced in me. I had an established career in law enforcement and attained the three-hat position of the sheriff's department personnel, legal and affirmative action officer. While working at headquarters, I was exposed to the dark side of politics in the department and in county government.

It didn't take long for my naive bubble to burst when I discovered that the sheriff wanted me to find a legal way around a recent court decision prohibiting him from summarily firing people without due process. And though I was the affirmation action officer, I was told not to take any affirmative action beyond going through the motions of getting the department off probation. It took even less time for me to realize that the sheriff, known as the "J. Edgar Hoover" of the county, maintained dual personnel files and intelligence files on everyone from city council members to county supervisors and judges. Anyone of power, wealth and influence in the county carried one of his badges.

With some encouragement from others in the department, in 1978 – the year of California's Proposition 13 tax revolt – I ran against my boss. He was a 25-year unopposed county sheriff, who abdicated his responsibility and abandoned our department and the citizens of the county to political infighting among his potential successors. Though unsuccessful, my family and I received a brutal education in dirty reality of political campaigns. My candidacy did, however, cause the sheriff to step down after the term. In time, the effort helped to accomplish many of the needed changes and improvements for the department and the county.

I continued my political education in 1980 by running for county supervisor to improve conditions in my district, which is very large and difficult to represent. My chances of being elected looked promising because I had done well in the district when I ran for sheriff. I campaigned on making county government accountable and more responsive. And I thought about how more democracy might improve representation. However, a wealthy landowner jumped in at the last moment and bought the election. My days of running for public office were over and my family couldn't have been happier.

Since I had been transferred to the county jail as a "political prisoner" just 3 days after announcing my candidacy for sheriff, my days in law enforcement were also over. I resigned shortly after losing the supervisor election. It was time for me to get out anyway. Sheriffs and police chiefs had far too much political power. Law enforcement dynasties were corrupt. And the new breed of young cops was disturbing. Too many of them were the first products of an aggressive, irresponsible generation.

Gross conflicts of interest caught up with the land baron who bought the 1980 supervisor's election. He was recalled after two years in office. Though I vowed never to run for office again, I did assist the recall candidate who succeeded him by writing a campaign platform that was responsible for getting him elected.

Voters were encouraged by the campaign platform because it was based upon a form of direct democracy for the candidate's constituents. The idea was to have citizen advisory councils comprised of members from every element of each community, selected by the people from those elements, not political appointees.

The Community Council concept was designed to give some direction to the supervisor as their representative and to provide a conduit for him to keep communities in the district informed about county government, including a complete accounting of their tax dollars. In addition, the council concept would provide the elements of each community with a communications medium to better understand each other's problems and concerns, and the ability to establish their priorities.

Unfortunately, like most people who become politicians, the supervisor was seduced by county politics, bureaucrats and his new-found personal power. Under pressure from the communities, he reluctantly formed several community councils. But after his election to a full term he made it painfully clear that he didn't want to be told what to do by the people in his district. The supervisor was soundly defeated in his bid for re-election. And the frustrating cycle of failures in representation continued. Fortunately, the current supervisor is competent young man who seems to grasp what it takes to do a good job.

After working for several years as the lead dispatcher for a joint powers communications center serving 5 fire departments, I learned how well city, county, state and federal fire agencies could work together, something rare among law enforcement agencies and departments. I also gained an education in city government and politics.

Then in 1985 I returned to work for San Bernardino County as a public defender investigator. While in law enforcement I earned a law degree so that I would know as much as lawyers in the system. But I did not go on to become a practicing attorney because I was simply incompatible with lawyers and their closed, questionable legal communities that were growing less and less desirable for someone like me.

The one thing that I learned from the law enforcement and legal professions was that they are both "closed communities." Law enforcement is closed within what could be called the "brotherhood of cops" because they are conditioned not to trust anyone but their own. The legal profession is a loosely knit brotherhood haunted by the constant conflict between doing the right thing and the "what's in it for me?" syndrome.

I have no problem working with lawyers in the criminal justice system. They are good, dedicated people and they have a tough, demanding job to do. I worked well with prosecutors and now defense attorneys, but I simply could not be one of them, rigidly confined to a cumbersome court system. Yet I had come full circle. I retired. And through it all, I've always maintained a particular interest in constitutional law.

The fire of democracy was rekindled in me in early 1991. I began watching politics and government on a larger scale and realized how dangerously our system had eroded. I wondered how the people could possibly bring about change in government so large, so remote, yet so entrenched in our lives. While writing *Black Robes on White Horses,"* a novel about the Supreme Court gaining too much power, I came up with the idea of direct democracy voting networks connected to voters' homes as the solution to runaway government. It had to be something more than merely responding to manipulated elections with predictable results.

Later that year, under the pseudonym of John Citizen, I took a giant leap by writing a small pamphlet proposing an amendment to the Constitution that would establish direct democracy. The proposal would enable citizens to control of government with direct democracy. It would establish a genuine government by the people.

The proposed 28th Amendment was intended to update and fix the Constitution and to provide voters with a method of communications to better understand each other's problems, concerns and priorities.

Then the presidential election year of 1992 rolled-in on the back of a recession. The opposing players were type-cast the same as the 1980 election when Ronald Reagan took the presidency away from recession-plagued Jimmy Carter. This time, however, they're roles would be reversed, not because of the recession, but because of a bee in the ointment that would turn into a political swarm.

Ross Perot buzzed onto the scene with an appearance on CNN's Larry King Live. Perot caught the people's attention with his billionaire status and his proposition that "The people are the owners of the country." The corny little guy touched a national nerve and created an overnight sensation when he promised that, if the people put him on the ballot in all 50 states, he would put on a "world class" campaign and help them take back the country from a government in default.

All the political pundits were confused, uneasy and often unnerved from the phenomenal public response to Perot and his call for volunteers to take up their voting arms. I was encouraged by his direct democracy concept of an "Electronic Town Hall" laser-beamed to the White House so the people could give him direction as their servant.

I was more impressed by the spontaneous national response to a figure of hope. People actually got out and participated in democracy by getting Perot on the ballot in all 50 states. Charged with enthusiasm, I re-directed my efforts to sending Perot a flow of information about the 28th Amendment and voting networks that would truly put all political power in the hands of the people.

But I got absolutely no response other than an indirect offer to be a volunteer. In the end, Perot served only to frustrate and confuse his devoted volunteers. He betrayed the people by his in-and-out and then back-in candidacy for president, his deceitful personal agenda and his hunger to be "King of America."

Two months before Election Day, I published and distributed the proposed 28th Amendment pamphlet. I sent copies to all the candidates for president, the leaders of Congress, the governors and legislatures of every state and the mainstream press.

During those efforts I didn't know much about Thomas Paine and the vital part he played the American Revolution. I didn't know about his writing and the publishing of *Common Sense*. I didn't know that Paine first wrote his pamphlet under the name of *an Englishman,* and had it published at his own expense.

1992 was an election year of unusual discontent and I was certain the idea of the 28th Amendment would surface, somewhere, somehow. But there was no response from anyone. Even my own Congressman did not reply until I confronted him with a personal letter. His response was a pat on the head, while condescending to me that it was a "novel idea." I was even more astonished by the eerie silence of the media, then I realized they simply don't pay any attention to common people unless there's something outrageous or zoo-like attached to it. Something for them to feed upon.

Perot left us with a legacy that he and we would come to regret. Arkansas Governor Bill Clinton slipped into the presidency. Perot could not abide the dark side of politics coming at him. When he perceived that President Bush and his campaign for re-election were playing dirty, he threw enough support to Bill Clinton to hand him the election with only 43 percent of the vote.

In an election as important as the presidency of the United States, no one should be elected to that office with less than a 50 percent plus one vote majority. If there hadn't been a 12th Amendment and the Electoral College there would have and should have been a run-off election. The 12th Amendment should have been repealed long ago. The election of the president should be by popular vote, and the matter should have been included in the 17th Amendment when the election of U.S. senators was changed to popular vote in 1913.

Ross Perot did, however, play an unwitting role in stimulating an effort to complete the American Revolution. He opened a door for the people to organize, exercise democracy and be heard in the political process of voicing their opinions about public policy. It cost Perot millions to open that door, but he slammed it shut with his inconsistent moods and his obsessions for domination and control. Somehow, Perot reminded me of that supervisor who was all for democracy until it came to yielding his power.

Nevertheless, like the few communities in my district, millions of voters tasted real democracy, if only for a brief time. The question remaining was, would it serve as a lasting passion for self-government? In the aftermath, Perot left his volunteers with the organization of United We Stand America to influence candidates, elections and public policy. The National Patriot Party was formed from other elements of his volunteers. Then Perot formed the Reform Party and ran again in 1996, but the people had lost interest in the little fraud with a big mouth.

We cannot overlook another powerful indicator of a rooting revolution. Rush Limbaugh. His booming radio voice has fired-up the minds of what millions of people are thinking. Limbaugh has become a monument to the conservative Republican agenda and a daily reminder of the evils inherent in the big liberal government of Democrats and the liberal mainstream press.

Limbaugh's success spawned a multitude of conservative hosts in the rising power of talk radio.

Like Perot, Limbaugh's philosophy was powerfully inviting. Also like Perot, I sent Limbaugh information about the 28th Amendment and the people's voting network, with no response. Neither Perot,

Limbaugh, nor anyone with real power would be willing to give it up to the people, including the national media.

Sadly, I realized that the media was hardened by the lust for rating dollars and status. They were obsessed with elite politics and celebrities, real, created or imagined, simply because it sells. Their corporate owners abandoned their responsibilities under the privileges of the First Amendment for the sake of profits. The media just wasn't concerned about the public interest in freedom and democracy, only its own liberal agenda. It's no wonder our citizens feel so helpless, disenfranchised and alone.

Knowing that California had always been on the cutting edge of political revolution, I began looking into an effort to place a constitutional initiative on the ballot that would establish direct democracy with a secure electronic voting network. I thought, if direct democracy could be established in California, other states would follow.

While studying the California Constitution, I was drawn to Article II. *Voting, Initiative and Referendum, and Recall.* Curiously, Section 1 [Purpose of Government] declares that "All political power is inherent in the people. Government is instituted for their protection, security and benefit, and they have the right to alter or reform it when the public good may require." Sounds good. Just like a democratic republic.

But it doesn't work that way. I soon realized the California Constitution was extremely complex. Ballot initiatives and referendums were not designed for the people because the process is too costly, restrictive and self-defeating for most citizens even to attempt. Rather, it's dominated by powerful moneyed special interests and the legislature. They play with people's minds and sell them out with deceitful ballot measures. Whenever a real people's initiative does pass, it is often circumvented by government, litigated against by special interests, or invalidated by the courts.

Depressed by the realization that so many people had lost the will to think about the true circumstances in which they live, I found it difficult to understand how people had become conditioned to selfish interests and dependency. How they'd come to expect government to fix everything. And how marginalized democracy was.

It took me a while to regain my determination and to renew my efforts to get the message out. During the California ballot initiative attempt, I solicited support from taxpayer and public interest groups such as the Howard Jarvis and Gann organizations of California Proposition 13 tax revolt fame that spread across the country. They were intrigued by the idea, however, they declined to assist because they had limited resources committed to specialized tax-related efforts. I sensed they wished it could happen, but there was a bitter flavor of futility in their responses.

Understandably, partisan politics, big government and large corporate interests including the media have reason to fear the idea of direct democracy. It would be terrifying for them to know that they could lose control of the country to the people. After all, they do have vested interests in choking off the voice of the people, keeping us ignorant, mute and conditioned to accept being insignificant.

I was so caught-up in the passions of my convictions that I didn't know how deeply low-esteem had been ingrained in the minds of the people. When acquaintances read the idea they agreed with the concept, but conceded that "They," meaning corporate and government power, would never let it happen.

Some displayed their lack of confidence in the people accepting the responsibility of direct democracy. Others felt that the public was too ignorant and irresponsible to handle it. Though their responses were discouraging I sensed a spark in their eyes telling me that they hoped for it to happen.

When I explained to them that their doubts were understood because there has been no credible experience with direct democracy since the birth of democracy in Athens, Greece 2500 years ago. And when I told them about the political power over taxation and public policy they could have at their fingertips, nearly all of them felt a sense of urgency for direct democracy.

In my first attempt to circulate a proposed 28th Amendment, I detailed everything I could think of about revising the Constitution. Since then, I've condensed and simplified the proposal, which included a proposal for direct education because I felt it was nearly as important to our future as direct democracy. I thought anyone could easily conclude that computers, telecommunications and information technology would dominate our future. The question remained, would we control it or would it control us? It was time to decide. Our future would depend on it.

It was also time for me to make a decision. Encouraged by my daughter, I gave up my typewriter and bought my first computer with a word processor. But how could I write on a computer? It was so complicated and distracting, how could I concentrate? Now, I can't imagine how I wrote so much on a typewriter or ever going back to using one. From that point on, I became a social, economic, technology, education and political observer, determined to speak out against our declining society and in favor of a better America. And, of course, I established a Website to promote direct democracy – something most people in power fear, for fear of losing power.

THE STRUGGLE TO BE HEARD

The failure of the two-party system and the 1992 Ross Perot candidacy for president caused me to change my voter registration from Republican to nonpartisan independent. I was a moderate, detested by leftwing liberals such as Ted Kennedy and rightwing conservatives such as Rush Limbaugh who believe that moderates stand for nothing. But, along with millions of other moderates who participated in democracy to get Perot elected, I became a passionate moderate determined to be heard.

Frustration filled my mind as I stared at the blank page in front of me. It was 1993 and I felt a deep sense of betrayal. Ross Perot handed the election to Bill Clinton out of spite for President Bush. I lost all the equity in my home, and it was worth less than my mortgage because of the recession and a steep decline in the real estate market. The American people seemed to have lost the will to fight for the kind of real democracy promised by Perot, and I was about to write my first letter to the editor of our local newspaper to vent my anger. I have since forgotten what it was about.

Anyway, I wrote the letter and sent it off in the mail. I kept writing letters to my local and regional newspapers, but couldn't seem to get any of them published. Then I began to read other people's letters, hoping to get a feel for the content of letters that had the best chance of making it to the printed page. Still, my letters got no response from the editors.

Soon I realized that published letters to the editor were not as hostile as mine, and they were writing about things they read in the newspaper, including other people's letters. So I took a lesson from that and finally got a letter or two published. When my regional newspaper, The San Bernardino Sun, published a commentary that I submitted to a column called, "It's Your Turn," I finally felt that I was on my way to being heard.

While writing my first novel, I was told to write about what I know. I had a brutal education about politics and government. I knew about the criminal justice system. And I experienced the troubling failure of public education and the disturbing decline of society. So I began to write letters about current events that I knew about and other things I was concerned about. I also learned that editors responded to letters that grabbed their attention, beginning and ending with "hook" sentences, which was a little something I picked up from lessons on creative writing.

In 1995, I decided to expand my letter writing to larger audiences, so I began writing letters to major newspapers and newsmagazines. It took a while, but on August 31, 1995, USA TODAY published my letter about the information technology revolution and direct democracy. I was further encouraged when USA TODAY published another letter about home education on September 19, 1995, and yet another letter about education in December. It was like a shot of adrenaline to me when America's only national newspaper published my letters. However, it was short-lived and I wouldn't get another letter published for over a year.

Meanwhile, I kept the letters going. My local and regional newspapers published many of them, and I was gaining somewhat of a reputation for speaking out about things other people were thinking strongly about. My friends, family, co-workers and many other people I knew agreed with my letters and brought it to my attention when they hadn't seen one lately because they looked forward to reading them.

By 1996, I had one letter published in TIME magazine, two in the Washington Times, and one in the Los Angeles Times. Then I decided to go for what I called a "Grand Slam" of published letters. At least one letter published in the five top print media: USA TODAY, The New York Times, The Washington Post, The Los Angeles Times and TIME Magazine. I had achieved three out of five. The New York Times and The Washington Post would prove to be the most difficult. Eventually, I would make the grand slam several times over.

Though I'm not a highly skilled writer, I found that ordinary people understood and responded to plain language rather than condescending, intellectual drivel. I also found that my increasing success in getting letters published would be the result of improving my writing by writing as often and as much as I could. And I found it interesting that New York Times and Washington Post editors would not publish a letter from a "commoner" unless it was very brief and edited by them.

It wasn't until 1998 that I got a letter published in the Washington Post, which was about John Glenn going back in space. Then in 1999, the grand slam was complete with a letter published in the New York Times and another in the Washington Post. The Washington Times – the other Washington newspaper – began publishing more and more of my letters, and it seemed as though I was their West Coast correspondent. That is, until they cut me off when the 2000 presidential elections rolled around, the stock market and the economy went sour, and I was writing too much about democracy and against the two-party system.

However, USA TODAY picked up on many of my letters and published them through the remainder of 1999, all of 2000 and the presidential election farce, and into 2001. Those were good letter-writing years. Several more were published in the Los Angeles Times, TIME Magazine and U.S. News & World Report. Of course I was still getting letters published in my local and regional newspapers.

After the September 11, 2001 attack on America, the competition to be heard was fierce. Everything changed. People and society, even government and politics seemed to change for the better, at least for a while. But the encouraging trend wouldn't last. After the stock market bubble burst – and the distraction of the retaliatory War in Afghanistan was over – corporate corruption was exposed and politics as usual reared its ugly head again during the 2002 elections. Then again over the controversial war in Iraq, and into the 2004 presidential election cycle, the social and political war games were well underway…

The struggle to be heard is an endless, particularly for the vast majority of people in every city, county and state in America. Most people are too busy working, raising families and trying to survive in a stressed-out society steeped in uncertainty. Too many people are resigned to believing they can't do anything to change things when they see something wrong. But this is a new era of information technology. Learn to write well enough to express your views and ideas simply and concisely, and you will be heard. If not in the newspaper, you can express yourself by writing letters to television news programs, radio programs or over the Internet in chat rooms, blog sites and to the expanding new media.

The information technology revolution and the age of new media have extended the opportunity for many more people to express themselves. Even television news programming has caught on to asking for and publishing more and more of people's letters – *The Fox News Channel* and Bill O'Reilly's "folks," for example. O'Reilly published a total of four of my e-mails and commented on them.

My first nonfiction book, *America's Crisis: The Direct Democracy and Direct Education Solution* was published in September 2000. It was featured on *C-Span BookTV* in early 2001. Some of the positive feedback I received was about the 25 letters to the editor I included at the end of the book, thus, the idea for writing and compiling the first letters to the editor book. *Letters to the Editor: From the Trenches of Democracy* published in 2005 was written for a large audience of moderate independents, squeezed uncomfortably between liberals and conservatives, who feel disenfranchised with little to no voice or power. That is, until it comes to being a consumer of goods and politics. And we all know that those in power are either trying to sell us something we don't need or to make money or to pander to us with lies and deceit to get elected or to stay in office. I felt the first letters book could help turn that around on them. Published or not, editors take serious note of what people have to say in their letters.

I retired in 2006, after a total of 41 years working in the criminal justice system. I served for 7 years with the Los Angeles County Sheriff's Department, 13 years with the San Bernardino County Sheriff's Department, and 21 years as a San Bernardino County Public Defender Investigator. After retiring, I served as a member of the 2007-2008 San Bernardino County Grand Jury -- and again in 2010-2011 -- which was an even more enlightening experience, delving into public corruption within county government. After my service on the Grand Jury, which resulted in the prosecution of the county assessor, a developer a city councilman and others, I began compiling Volume 2 of Letters to the Editor.

After Volume 2 was published, I compiled my unpublished letters to the editor into Volume 3, after which Volume 4 was published and I began compiling Volume 5.

THE MEDIA CENSORS IMPORTANT
LETTERS THAT DON'T FIT ITS CULTURE

I have been fortunate to have a number of letters published in major newspapers and news magazines -- such as USA TODAY, The New York Times, Washington Post, Washington Times, Washington Examiner, Los Angeles Times, San Diego Union-Tribune, San Francisco Chronicle, Time Magazine and US News & World Report -- regarding a variety of social, political and economic issues or events.

However, to get my letters published I have had to restrict my comments to current media sensations, acceptable tie-ins to news reports, editorials or commentary, and to limit my criticism to that which fits the media's ideology. Indeed, when it comes to the importance of pointing out the damage extreme feminism has done to relationships, families, men, women and children; or commenting on the divisiveness, hate and discontent perpetuated by the selfish interests of racial activists and the diversity culture; or condemning the academic establishment for robbing generations of students of their education; or criticizing the media culture, which suffers from the unintended consequences of cloaking itself in bias – such letters and the needed balance of views and dialogue from people outside the culture's parochial parameters are deemed politically incorrect, heavily edited, censored or simply ignored.

Unfortunately, with few exceptions, television news media are worse, even more condescending and detached from reality, and they don't or won't share people's feedback unless it fits into their way of thinking (*C-Span* not included). Any doubts were dispelled when I witnessed *New York Times* columnist Maureen Dowd's snide and awkward comparisons of President Bush and Tom Brokaw at the National Press Club's 2003 Fourth Estate Award dinner for the *NBC Nightly News* anchor (held 11-19-03 and subsequently aired on *C-Span*). Dowd's veiled attempt at humor seemingly entertained the media elite in attendance, but she was typically arrogant and about as subtle and satirical as political train-wrecks, Al Franken and Michael Moore.

Most people are informed about what's supposedly going on around them by what they read, see and hear from the major news media. Yet it's troubling to know how reticent the media is about impartial objectivity. And it's troubling to know that many important issues and events are intentionally under-reported or unaddressed, and that most people are unapprised of vital information. It's even more troubling that freedom of the press is a constitutional guarantee, and the media vigorously defends that right, yet they (often unwittingly) censor the very people they are supposed to watch out for and defend. I guess CBS whistleblower (author of *Bias: How the Media Distort the News*) Bernard Goldberg is correct, and that's highly disturbing.

Certainly, glaring examples of bias and censorship have been manifested by media's partisan coverage of the war against terrorism since the September 11, 2001 attack on America and, currently, the war in Iraq. It's frightening to observe how the media consistently attacked President Bush and his administration with anti-war themes, negative reporting and undermining the morale of the military and the people, while failing to report and call former president Clinton and his administration to account for his lack of action against terrorism leading to the attack on America. Surely, our security and our future – and the betrayal of democracy, education and the core of America's culture – is the heavy price society is already paying...

As if the attack on America and the war against terrorism wasn't enough for the nation to endure, the Democrat takeover of Congress in 2006, and the 2008 election of Barack Obama as president, while finance, housing and the economy were imploding, would prove even more disastrous. Though President Bush pushed for reforming Fannie Mae and Freddie Mac, Congress resisted and it was too little, too late.

The root of the crash was forced affordable housing that began with the Carter administration's Community Reinvestment Act. Which was used by the Clinton administration to intimidate banks and mortgage lenders to lower their standards and give home loans to those who could not afford them. Unaffordable housing expanded rapidly throughout the government-backed mortgage securities and finance industry until the bubble burst.

Of course, the collapsing economy, job losses, home foreclosures and bankruptcies were exacerbated by President Obama and the Democrat-controlled Congress passing a wasted $800 billion stimulus bill, national health careless laws, finance regulations and $7 trillion in deficit spending, sending the national debt soaring to over $18 trillion, and pushing us to the fiscal cliff of insolvency.

Alas, none of it will matter if Mr. Obama's abdication of his national security responsibilities, surrendering to the proliferation of the Islamic terrorism of ISIS, al-Qaeda, Iran's expansion and nuclear threat result in all out attacks on Israel, America and the West.

Oops! Now, even though this one was a little hostile and much too long, my letters might be blacklisted. But at least I got it off my chest. Hopefully, my published and unpublished letters will help explain my take on the social, political, economic and national security issues over the past 20 years. Hopefully, the following tips on letter writing will help you express your views, whatever they may be....

TIPS ON LETTER WRITING

Letters to the editor are unique to the newspaper and newsmagazine business. Our history of letters to the editor in the United States date back to the American Revolution. Indeed, the Federalist and Anti-Federalist Papers consisted of letters to the editor from several of our Founders during the constitutional debates.

Newspapers generally use letters to the editor as a public forum for reader reaction to published information on current events. Letters regarding issues that interest opinion and editorial page (Op-Ed) editors are most likely to be published, and that happens to be the first lesson on letter writing.

PICK AN ISSUE

Read editorials and letters to the editor in your newspaper to give you a feel for what editors are looking for. Use other people's letters as a guide to how they approach issues. Editors prefer to see a reference to something in their newspapers. If a letter writer does not refer to an editorial, previous article, commentary or letter, the editor will usually include a reference to the issue.

If an event published in the newspaper grabs your interest or an issue stirs your concerns, that is what you should write about. However, don't write when you are angry. Believe me, it seldom comes out convincing or readable.

Published reports, articles and commentary on issues or events of the day or the week are what editors focus on. Therefore, well-composed letters about major issues and events stand the best chance of being published.

Only a few letters make it past the "tie-in" or "tag" test to stand alone. My unusual "State of the Union" letter published in USA TODAY on September 17, 1997 is one such letter.

Pick a side

If an issue or event is the subject of public debate in the media and you feel strongly about it, one way or the other, pick a side and write a letter. You will stand a better chance of your letter being published if you add something fresh and different to the debate that will interest editors and readers. Sometimes that fresh difference stems from an opinion from the center of an important issue or event.

Letters from the center

Published social, political and economic letters to the editor are dominated by letter writers from the left and right with liberal or conservative bias, even though most people's viewpoints come from the center. In other words, the majority of Americans are moderate centrists.

However, people from the center write fewer letters to editor simply because they are the least active in voicing their opinions about social, political and economic events and issues. On some issues they lean to the left and on other issues they lean to the right. Most centrists identify themselves as leaning socially liberal and fiscally conservative.

I happen to be an independent, moderate centrist who is politically and socially active. Unfortunately, people like me are somewhat rare because of the very nature of moderate label. Actually, I could be described as a "radical" moderate. Contrary to the way it sounds, it is not an oxymoron.

Nevertheless, my centrist approach to writing letters to the editor has contributed to my success in getting letters published, not because the letters are so well written, but because fewer letters from centrists are received by editors and that makes them fresh and different.

HOWEVER

Since Democrats took over the Congress, the economic crash, and the election of Barack Obama, there has been a new awakening in America, including me. When the economic pain hits home, people re-evaluate themselves. Now I, along with the majority of Americans, consider ourselves socially and politically center-right. And as the pain increases, we are moving further to the conservative side.

Bill O'Reilly is a perfect example of a center-right independent. He and Fox News offered the fair and balanced truth in news, and there is a new sheriff in town.

The 2010 mid-term elections proved that by Republicans taking over the House, with gains in the Senate, and throughout state governments. What we need next is control of the Senate and another Ronald Reagan in the White House. A tall order since Reagan was an American original – one of the kind….

That order could have been filled by Mitt Romney and Rep. Paul Ryan in the 2012 presidential election, but with liberal press continuing to back President Obama, he was re-elected.

Learn from journalists

Read articles that interest you, which are written by staff reporters, and examine how they construct their writing. Do the same with Associated Press (AP) articles that have an AP reporter's by-line. Finally, review how editorial writers and columnists present their writing. You can learn from professionals by paying particular attention to the way they begin and end each paragraph.

Begin and end with a "hook"

If you want to catch an editor's eye, you should begin your letter with a hook and end it with a hook. State the problem and offer a solution or conclusion that is likely to grab the editor's interest. The reasons are obvious. Neither editors nor readers will read uninteresting letters.

Likewise, you should begin and end each paragraph in the body of the letter with hook sentences, especially if you want to get a longer letter published. Below are examples of hooks about the "energy crisis" issue:

First sentence hook:

The energy crisis should not have happened, but it did, and we've got government's lack of sound energy policy and corporate greed to thank for it.

Last sentence hook:

Maybe it's time for the people to own and operate "public utilities."

Keep it simple, concise and to the point – "pithy"

Most newspapers limit letters to between 150 and 300 words. However, many local newspapers publish longer letters if they are well written, or they simply don't have anything better to publish and they need to fill space.

If large newspaper editors like your "hooks," they will edit your letter to fit the available space. I wrote one lengthy letter that was published by using only the first and last paragraphs because they contained good "hooks."

Major papers like the New York Times and the Washington Post edit nearly all of their letters for length, style and content. It seems they don't believe many of us are capable of writing a letter to publish, as-is. At least that has been my experience. And that is why it's important to make your points in the first, middle and last paragraphs.

Not all editors reply to letter submissions, but it doesn't really matter. The only contact that means anything is a request for letter confirmation from someone on the editorial staff. That usually means they are going to publish your letter.

Control the rhetoric

Among other things, rhetoric is defined as the art of effective expression and the persuasive use of language. It is also defined as affected or pretentious language such as political rhetoric. When writing letters to the editor, it is suggested that you control your rhetoric. Do not cross the line from the effective expression of your views to pretentious or inflammatory political rhetoric.

Further, when you feel so strongly about something that you come off sounding like a raving zealot, editors will certainly shy away from your letter. As you read my letters you will notice that I often push that fine line between effective expression and political rhetoric. The trick is to keep it toned down enough to keep it from crossing the line.

Make it interesting

Your point of view should be interesting and educational to the editor and readers. If you are challenging something or someone with opposing facts, be certain to do your homework. You shouldn't just say someone is full of it without backing it up. The best letters that I have read contained something I didn't know.

Say what others are thinking

Editors know when someone writes a letter that says what many readers are thinking. Keep that in mind when you write your letter. Those other people will thank you for it.

Give your letter a title

The best way to grab an editor's attention is with a good title. The title should convey the theme of the letter in a few words similar to newspaper headlines. Editors seldom, if ever, use your title but that's what makes them read your letter over other letters because you're speaking their language.

Reference your letter

As indicated above, if you are writing about something that you read in a newspaper or newsmagazine, make reference to the article, editorial, commentary or letter that you are responding to.

You will have a much better chance at getting your letter published if you join or begin a debate on a major local, state or national issue that is widely published.

Edit and revise your letter

Except for my wife, I don't know anyone who can write a good letter without editing and revising it. I've tried and it seldom works. After you have written the first draft, walk away. Then come back later and read it. You'll often find that it doesn't read nearly as well as you thought when you first wrote it. You may even need to leave it until the next day to re-work it.

Read the letter aloud to yourself or have someone else read it to you to hear how it sounds. If it's easy to read and understand it will probably gain more consideration from editors, and it will be more attractive to your intended audience. Above all, make sure the spelling is correct and that you have condensed the letter as much as possible.

Don't use too many "big words."

If you use too many big words readers might think you're talking down to them. That offends many people and others simply won't be able to understand your message.

One or two well-placed $25 words, however, often helps to drive home your point, and it also attracts the attention of editors.

Timely letters

If you are going to comment on an issue in the news, jump on it while it's hot. With word processors and e-mail, it's much easier to get a letter off to the editor. Most newspapers and newsmagazines accept letters by e-mail. And remember include your address and phone number.

FROM THE TRENCHES OF DEMOCRACY

You may or may not agree with the social, political and economic commentary contained in my letters to the editor. But you will probably agree that letters to the editor are one of the few trenches of democracy from where our voices can be heard by large audiences. Your views regarding local, state, national and global issues are what you should write about.

Call-in radio and television shows provide other mediums to voice your opinion, however, most of them are screened and limited to only a few callers. *C-Span* is unequaled in offering nonpartisan and uncensored telephone access to speak your mind to a great many viewers and listeners throughout the nation.

Fortunately, more and more people are practicing democracy wherever they find it. The Internet has opened up even more avenues. E-mail, forums, conferences, message boards, chat rooms and blog sites offer much more access than ever before.

The media have taken to the Internet with on-line versions of newspapers, radio and television news. Most of them offer access for writing letters to the editor by e-mail. But some limit letters to form submissions. Don't try to write a letter on-line. Compose your letter off-line, then copy and paste it for an on-line submission. You should do the same when posting any lengthy submission.

Television news has grown from brief morning programs and 15 minutes of evening news (50 years ago) to 24 hour instant news. News on the "tube" has become highly competitive. Cable and broadcast news networks pump out whatever they think improves their ratings regardless of how newsworthy it is.

Rather than providing responsible journalism, television news has turned into superficial reporting, entertainment and shock media. Journalistic integrity has been replaced by celebrity journalists and a "chattering class" of pundits.

What was once known as the people's "watch-dogs" has turned into the fame business, condescending elitists, biased politics and rating races. Even though most people get their news from television, the public's trust in television news and much of the print media has plummeted.

ABC, CBS, NBC and CNN are the most biased and the worst violators of the public trust. **ABC**, however, took a leap in the right direction with *20/20's* "Give Me a Break" reporter, John Stossel. His specials exposing the troubling fraud of extreme environmentalism in our schools, the disturbing August 4, 2001 report on America's "Hype" society and the August 11, 2001 report on "Washington" demonstrated ABC's trend-bucking lean in the direction of more responsible journalism.

I wrote a letter ABC commending Stossel and the news division for his special reports. But it didn't last. Stossel took a lot of heat from the liberal establishment, and he was eventually cast out. Even so, he stood fast with his contribution of a series of programs for schools and education. Now, John Stossel has a home with his own show on the Fox News Business Channel.

Still, when it comes to criticism the news media does not take it very well. Indeed, they give it little more than superficial lip service among themselves from time to time. In the end, however, most of the dominant news media usually just ignore it from their lofty, out-of-touch, perches.

But if we persist in writing well-composed letters we can get their attention. If you want to make an impact, write your letters and send your e-mails to the broadcast networks, cable channels, and to their sponsors. Corporate owners of the news business focus on bottom line profits. Social responsibility is the last thing on their minds.

Therefore, the only way to get their attention is by audience complaints and pressure on their corporate advertisers.

Elected representatives usually respond to all letters from their constituents. Unfortunately, their responses are usually shallow pats on the head for being a good, concerned citizen along with a political propaganda pitch. But if they are inundated with a flood of letters and phone calls it does makes a difference, simply because they're always worried about being re-elected.

When writing letters to government agency bureaucrats, especially with complaints, you should address your letter to the head of the agency. It is also helpful to send copies of your letter to your elected representatives and indicate that copies were sent. Many of those department heads are appointed by elected officials.

Writing effective letters can also help you in dealing with personal and business problems including, but not limited to, insurance companies, health care providers, utility companies, banks, credit card companies, lawyers, contractors, and any other business or entity with which you are a client, patient or customer.

Just remember one thing. When writing that letter, start at the top with the president, CEO, manager or business owner. It is much easier than trudging through layers of bureaucracy. You might not get a personal response, but you should get an answer from someone not far down from the top. Even if you don't get a response, rest assured that most letters have some effect.

If you're upset about something, write a letter. It's likely that other people are also upset and have written letters that could have a cumulative effect, which should get someone's attention.

Other than conducting selective polls that only capture people's responses to snapshots about issues, the news media, government and corporate America are woefully out of touch with the people. They are simply clueless about what it's really like out here in the trenches of democracy.

What angers and frustrates most people is being ignored. But if you're persistent in writing effective letters your message will get through. It is my hope and objective to assist you in being heard. **That's what democracy is all about...**

Pep talk

America is hurting and that means us. It's time to re-examine ourselves and do something to make a difference. Though we all have much to deal with in our lives, not much changes unless we make it happen. Many of us feel disenfranchised from government and society.

It is my intention to get you excited about participating in democracy. Get involved by reading books, newspapers and magazines. Watch the news from different sources on television, including *C-Span*. Search the Internet for different views and more information. And compare it all in an effort to find the truth, which seems to be so elusive these days.

Then write those letters. Share what you've learned to help other people find the truth. Write what you feel. Write for justice. Write against injustice. Write for change. Write to support something good. Write to defeat something bad. Complain and criticize, but make it constructive. Identify a problem, but try not to leave it hanging without offering a solution...

CITIZEN'S CORNER

Publish more letters

There is nothing more important or telling about a newspaper than how it handles letters to the editor from its readers.

Two of the most important civil liberties that we possess are "freedom of speech" and "freedom of the press" guaranteed by the First Amendment to the Constitution. It is "my opinion" that a free press should embrace citizens' free speech by publishing more letters to the editor which accurately reflect what is really on their readers' minds. Not just reactions to newspaper stories, editorials and commentary, but people's original thoughts, criticisms, ideas and suggestions.

Local newspapers and publications do a pretty good job of reflecting local opinion about matters of local interest, however, even they could do better. Larger newspapers, newsmagazines and publications have a long way to go to satisfy the public's need to communicate opinion to their fellow citizens, especially when the print media are merging into fewer, impersonal news media giants and conglomerates.

Here's a suggestion for the news media: In addition to publishing letters to the editor, newspaper and newsmagazine editors could select boards of contributors from citizen letter writers to establish what could be called a "Citizen's Corner" in their opinion and editorial sections. Rotating board members could field letters of public interest with brief commentary, which could also include letters of debate over people's legitimate concerns. Indeed, such an approach could go a long way in mending the fractured relationship between people's free speech and the free press — the public and the news media.

LIST OF NEWSPAPERS AND NEWSMAGAZINES

Total account of my published letters in Volumes 1, 2, 4 and 5

Major newspapers

USA TODAY	64 letters
Los Angeles Times	50 letters
Washington Post	4 letters
New York Times	11 letters
Washington Times	45 letters
Washington Examiner	49 letters
Wall Street Journal	5 letters
Boston Globe	2 letters
New York Post	22 letters
O'Reilly Factor	6 emails

National newsmagazines

Time Magazine	7 letters
U.S. NEWS & World Report	5 letters
Newsweek Magazine	1 letter

L. A. Times Magazine	1 letter
NewsMax Magazine	18 letters

Regional newspapers

The San Bernardino Sun	80 letters
Riverside Press-Enterprise	50 letters
San Diego Union-Tribune	
(and North County Times)	82 letters
San Francisco Examiner	12 letters
San Francisco Chronicle	8 letters
Sacramento Bee	7 letters
Orange County Register	3 letters

Local newspaper

Victor Valley Daily Press	
- Press Dispatch	118 letters
Apple Valley Review	22 commentaries

Total letters 671

LET'S BEGIN...

The following chapters (listed by year) contain my published and unpublished letters to the editor

Whether or not you agree with the observations and opinions contained in my letters, they should be informative. My letters are written snapshots in time addressing most of the major events and issues over the past 2 years, with emphasis on the 2014 mid-term elections, and my state of California. They are simply one person's take on recent social, economic and political history from the point of view of a common citizen with an uncommon passion.

I sincerely hope the letters will be of interest to you and that they will assist you in writing your own letters. Stay with it and you will get published. As you will see, my letters improved year after year. And as you will discover, there's nothing like seeing your letter in print and knowing that your voice has been heard.

CHAPTER 1

2013 - 2015 Letters

Riverside Press Enterprise
January 22, 2015

Obama's State of the Union fails to deliver

President Obama's state of the union speech was little more than preaching to the choir of Democrats, lecturing Republicans, taking credit for the improved economy and insisting on more regulation, taxing and spending. The truth is, the economy has improved not because of Mr. Obama, but in spite of him.

Alas, the president's sorry state of the union and his legacy is replete with government growth, enormous debt, economic stagnation and diminishing national security.

Hopefully, the economy won't collapse and America will not be rife with terrorism during President Obama's last two years in office.

Daniel B. Jeffs
Apple Valley

USA TODAY
January 22, 2015
Opinion – Your Say
State of the Union
(Lead letter with headline)

Is the economy better because of Obama or despite him?

President Obama's state of the union speech was little more than preaching to the choir of Democrats and lecturing Republicans. Obama took credit for the improved economy and backed more regulation, taxing and spending ("Obama pushes plans to hoist middle class," News, Wednesday),

The truth is, the economy has improved not because of Obama, but in despite him. Alas, the president's sorry speech and his legacy are replete with government growth, enormous debt, economic stagnation and diminishing national security.

Hopefully, the economy won't collapse and America will not be rife with terrorism during President Obama's last two years in office.

Daniel B. Jeffs
Apple Valley, Calif.

Riverside Press Enterprise
January 19, 2015

Call it what it is: Treason

An Ohio man, and radicalized Muslim convert, Christopher Cornell, was arrested for plotting to attack the capitol.

This is a treasonous plot to overthrow our government, but he will undoubtedly no be charged with treason. Others who should be charged with treason include Major Nidal Hasan, Sgt, Bowe Burgdahl, Pvt. Chelsea Manning, Edward Snowden, American Muslim imams who support arming the Islamic State in Iraq and Syria, and all the American citizens who went to fight with ISIS.

But they won't be.

This is particularly the case with President Obama and Attorney General Eric Holder in office, who fail to support and defend the Constitution and the United States against all enemies, foreign and domestic. No one has been charged with treason for many years.

Why?

This is a serious matter that should be looked into by our elected representatives and the media. Our survival is at stake.

Daniel B. Jeffs
Apple Valley

The Washington Times
January 13, 2015

Paris no-show matches rest of presidency

President Obama's failure last week to make an appearance joining world leaders in solidarity against the terrorist attacks in Paris highlighted six years of failed leadership ("Obama's snub of Paris," Jan, 12) This failure resulted in the unfettered growth of al Qaeda and Islamic State terrorists throughout the Middle East, Africa and the World, and puts America and the West at extreme risk.

Worse, the president's failure to secure Iraq and stop Iran from obtaining nuclear weapons, as well as its implicit permission of the Taliban to take Pakistan (which could result in Taliban takeover of Pakistan and the country's nuclear weapons) makes Israel, India and the United States vulnerable to nuclear attacks.

Indeed, Mr. Obama's failure to execute a firm plan to secure our borders and fight terrorism wherever it raises its evil head will likely result in small terrorist cells spread throughout the United States.

These cells could result in nationwide attacks on Americans. Hopefully, those terrorist cells are not already in place.

Toying with terrorism, coupled with the president's failure to maintain or increase our nuclear defenses and the defense of our allies makes it painfully clear Mr. Obama has abdicated his solemn responsibility to protect and defend our nation from all enemies, foreign and domestic.

Daniel B. Jeffs
Apple Valley, Calif.

Los Angeles Times
January 11, 2015

Alternative ways to go green

The Times' support of Gov. Brown's costly green agenda comes as no surprise. Indeed, it doesn't seem to matter how much damage the punishing cap and trade taxes will do to California's economy in terms of skyrocketing energy prices and the overall cost of living.

Coupled with all the damage California's U.S. Senator Barbara Boxer has done with her environmental extremist work against California, she and Gov. Brown have blindly driven California on a runaway train to crashing at the hands of regressive liberals.

Daniel B. Jeffs
Apple Valley, Calif.

(original letter)

Re: Gov. Brown's green agenda – editorial and Sen. Boxer's exit

The Los Angeles Times editorial board's support of Gov. Brown's costly green agenda comes as no surprise. Indeed, it doesn't seem to matter how much damage AB 32's punishing cap and trade taxes will do to California's economy or to the people of California in terms of skyrocketing energy prices and the overall cost of living. The L.A. Times supports it along with the Democrat Legislature in terms of global warming hoax and unreliable green energy.

Coupled with all the damage California's U.S. Senator Barbara Boxer has done with her environmental extremist work against California and the nation, Sen. Boxer and Gov. Brown have blindly driven California on a runaway train to crashing at the hands of regressive liberals. Alas, at least we can finally be rid of authoritarian hand when she leaves the Senate. Still, we will continue to be assaulted and battered by Gov. Brown's tax lies and high speed rail money pit.

Unfortunately, Sen. Boxer and soon-to-retire Sen. Feinstein will surely be replaced with the like infections of regressive Democrats elected by indoctrinated voters bent on committing voter-assisted social, political and economic suicide..

San Bernardino Sun
January 8, 2015

New year of life, liberty and pursuit of happiness

The best New Year's resolution would be for the American people to resolve to fight-off the socialist cancer metastasizing throughout the body of our society from the attacks against the Founders' traditional America, our Constitution and free markets, the abuse of power by big government – complicit news media and entertainment industry -- to badly misinformed parenting, to students being indoctrinated by the miseducation system in factories of ignorance, to anti-social media, and the relentless spread of mind-numbing propaganda and criminal behavior.

Indeed, 2015 should be embraced by getting our lives together for life, liberty, the pursuit of happiness -- and the defense of our domestic and national security freedom.

Daniel B. Jeffs
Apple Valley

VV Daily Press
December 29, 2014

Shared blame

Former New York City Police Commissioner Bernard Kerik should have included President Obama when he accused Mayor Bill De Blasio and Al Sharpton of having "blood on their hands" over Ismaaiyl Brinsley's execution of two NYPD officers in Brooklyn in retaliation for the deaths of Eric Garner and Michael Brown.

Indeed, New York City voters share that blame for electing a police-hating socialist mayor, as are U.S. voters for electing like-minded President Obama, who appointed Sharpton as his race-relations counselor and sent him to Ferguson, Missouri, then to New York to lead protests against police – deepening racial divisions – and weakening our first line of defense: The protection and service of law enforcement.

Daniel B. Jeffs
Apple Valley

(original letter)

NYPD officers executed
Former New York City Police Commissioner Bernard Kerik should have included President Obama when he accused Mayor De Blasio and Al Sharpton of having "blood on their hands" over Ismaaiyl

Brinsley's execution of two NYPD officers in Brooklyn in retaliation for the deaths of Eric Garner and Michael Brown.

Indeed, New York City voters share that blame for electing a police-hating socialist mayor, as are U.S. voters for electing like-minded President Obama, who appointed Sharpton as his race-relations counselor and sent him to Ferguson, Missouri, then to New York to lead protests against police – deepening racial divisions – and weakening our first line of defense: The protection and service of law enforcement.

As a former deputy sheriff, sergeant, personnel officer, public defender investigator and two-time grand jury member with 43 years of service, I witnessed and experienced the anti-establishment, anti-war counter-traditional-culture revolution and criminal law revolution from 1960's Watts Riots to the first decade of the 21st Century and the rise of terrorism.

Alas, it is deeply troubling to attest to reasons for the steep decline of America's domestic and national social, political and economic security – particularly, since the 2008 elections -- at the un-American hands of President Obama and the Democrat Congress. Surely, it's time for a traditional-culture revolution and the restoration of our land of the free and the home of the brave.

New York Times
December 10, 2014

Scathing report on C.I.A. torture

The release of the torture report raises fears, and it should. Senator Dianne Feinstein's reckless disregard for national security in her spite-ful release of the C.I.A. enhanced interrogation report – supported by President Obama -- will surely endanger our allies, American facilities and the lives of C.I.A. agents worldwide. This is particularly true in the current climate of fanatic terrorism by the Islamic State, Al Qaeda and other terrorist organizations.

This report is simply unconscionable partisan politics against the Bush administration's actions after the 9/11 attack on America.

(Original letter)

Senator Feinstein's ugly half-truth

The December 9, 2014 release of the torture report raises fears and it should. Supported by President Obama, outgoing Senate Intelligence Committee Chair, Dianne Feinstein's ugly half-truth and reckless disregard for national security in her spiteful release of the CIA enhanced interrogation report will surely endanger America, our allies, U.S facilities, the lives of CIA operatives and our troops throughout the world. Particularly, in the current, hostile climate of fanatic terrorism by ISIS, al Qaeda and other terrorist organizations.

Clearly, Feinstein's treasonous actions were based upon her Democrat lack of intelligence committee's staff hit-squad investigation, half-truths and without interviewing any of the parties involved. Senator McCain's personal experience clouding his judgment notwithstanding, Republicans on the committee refused to participate in Feinstein's vindictive kangaroo court for good reason. It's simply unconscionable partisan politics against the Bush administration's actions to protect us after the 9/11 attack on America.

As expected, President Obama's blindly-biased news media supports the release and report, which ignores the fact that the Bush Administration and CIA kept America safe, and their actions ultimately located Osama bin Laden, which resulted in his death.

San Diego Union-Tribune
December 10, 2014

Mixed reactions to torture report release
(lead letter)

The release of the torture report raises fears and it should.

Supported by President Obama, outgoing Senate Intelligence Committee Chair, Dianne Feinstein's reckless disregard for national security in her spiteful release of the CIA enhanced interrogation report will surely endanger America, our allies, U.S facilities, the lives of CIA agents worldwide.

Particularly, in the current climate of fanatic terrorism by ISIS, al Qaeda and other terrorist organizations. It's simply unconscionable partisan politics against the Bush administration's actions to protect us after the 9/11 attack on America.

(Original letter)
Senator Feinstein's ugly half-truth

The December 9, 2014 release of the torture report raises fears and it should. Supported by President Obama, outgoing Senate Intelligence Committee Chair, Dianne Feinstein's ugly half-truth and reckless disregard for national security in her spiteful release of the CIA enhanced interrogation report will surely endanger America, our allies, U.S facilities, the lives of CIA operatives and our troops throughout the world. Particularly, in the current, hostile climate of fanatic terrorism by ISIS, al Qaeda and other terrorist organizations.

Clearly, Feinstein's treasonous actions were based upon her Democrat lack of intelligence committee's staff hit-squad investigation, half-truths and without interviewing any of the parties involved. Senator McCain's personal experience clouding his judgment notwithstanding, Republicans on the committee refused to participate in Feinstein's vindictive kangaroo court for good reason. It's simply unconscionable partisan politics against the Bush administration's actions to protect us after the 9/11 attack on America.

As expected, President Obama's blindly-biased news media supports the release and report, which ignores the fact that the Bush Administration and CIA kept America safe, and their actions ultimately located Osama bin Laden, which resulted in his death.

VV Daily Press
November 26, 2014

Rejecting jobs

Last stand Democrats in the Senate blocked the passage of approving the Keystone XL oil pipeline, which would have created thousands of jobs and taken America much closer to energy independence. However, liberal Democrat arrogance delayed the passage until Republicans take over control of the Senate in January, leaving it for President Obama to approve or veto.

President Obama has unnecessarily delayed approving Keystone for nearly two years, which comes as no surprise. Mr. Obama has abused his executive order authority with edicts and declarations against oil, gas and coal energy, and for unreliable green energy since he was first elected. Note: It's time to stop the annoying phone calls pitching solar panels and windows to residential property owners.

Indeed, the president is more interested in pursuing the global warming hoax, which will cost taxpayers and make our electric bills "skyrocket," as he said in his 2008 run for the office. Worse, the blind pursuit of green energy will surely break the economic backs of business and the middle class -- and crush America's economy in the process.

Riverside Press Enterprise
November 22, 2014

Keystone bill's sad loss

Last stand Democrats in the Senate blocked the passage of approving the Keystone XL oil pipeline, which would have created thousands of jobs and taken America much closer to energy independence. However, liberal Democrat arrogance delayed the passage until Republicans take over control of the Senate in January, leaving it for President Obama to approve or veto it.

President Obama has unnecessarily delayed approving Keystone for nearly two years, which comes as no surprise. Mr. Obama has abused his executive order authority with edicts and declarations against oil, gas and coal energy, and for unreliable green energy since he was first elected. Note: It's time to stop the annoying phone calls pitching solar panels and windows to residential property owners.

Indeed, the president is more interested in pursuing the global warming hoax, which will cost taxpayers and make our electric bills "skyrocket," as he said in his 2008 run for the office. Worse, the blind pursuit of green energy will surely break the economic backs of business and the middle class -- and crush America's economy in the process.

San Diego Union-Tribune
November 21, 2014

Keystone letters round-up

Last-stand Democrats in the Senate blocked the passage of approving the Keystone XL oil pipeline, which would have created thousands of jobs and taken America much closer to energy independence.

However, liberal Democrat arrogance delayed the passage until Republicans take over control of the Senate in January, leaving it for President Obama to approve or veto.

President Obama has unnecessarily delayed approving Keystone for nearly two years, which comes as no surprise. Mr. Obama has abused his executive order authority with edicts and declarations against oil, gas and coal energy and for unreliable green energy since he was first elected.

Indeed, the president is more interested in pursuing the global warming hoax, which will cost taxpayers and make our electric bills "skyrocket," as he said in his 2008 run for office.

Worse, the blind pursuit of green energy will surely break the economic backs of business and the middle class and crush America's economy in the process.

NewsMax Magazine
November issue 2014

Obama's legacy

President Obama's speech to the United Nations confirms that he believes he is the world healer, while his domestic policy is ruining our economy and our freedoms. Indeed, Mr. Obama is betraying our national security while he fights the fires of terrorism with sticks, stones and a garden hose to finish his time in office. That will likely be the curse of President Obama's legacy ("Obama's new inner circle acts to bolster his legacy," September).

The Washington Times
October 16, 2014

Betrayal of Israel, Kurds has ramifications

President Obama has betrayed our only solid allies in the Middle East; namely, the Kurds and Israel. With the failures of the airstrike campaign against the Islamic State, Mr. Obama betrayed the Kurds by failing to provide arms and significant military support to fight these terrorists.

Indeed, Mr. Obama should have established a strong military base in Kurdistan.

Worse, the president has betrayed Israel by playing a dangerous one-sided game with Iran's insidious campaign to finish developing its nuclear weapons program, which will be used against Israel, America and the West.

Clearly, Mr. Obama's unconscionable inaction and serial dereliction of duty is inviting national security disasters upon Israel and terrorist acts against the United States at the hands of a nuclear Iran and Islamic State. Coupled with his failures vis-à-vis the growing threat of Russia to us and our NATO allies, he has put the entire world as risk.

San Bernardino Sun
October 15, 2014

Obama betrays our allies in the Middle East

President Obama has betrayed our only solid allies in the Middle East: The Kurds and Israel. With the failures of the air strike campaign against ISIS, President Obama betrayed the Kurds by failing to provide arms and significant military support to them for fighting ISIS.

Indeed, Mr. Obama should have established a strong military base in Kurdistan. Worse, the president has betrayed Israel by playing a dangerous one-sided game with Iran's insidious campaign to finish developing its nuclear weapon program, which will be used against Israel, America and the West.

Clearly, President Obama's unconscionable inaction and serial dereliction of duty is inviting national security disasters upon Israel and terrorist acts against the United States at the hands of a nuclear Iran and ISIS.

Coupled with the president's failures with Russia's growing threat America and our NATO allies, he has put the entire world as risk.

VV Daily Press
October 12, 2014

Whose monument?

President Obama's executive order to make the San Gabriel Mountains a national monument is not for the people, as it will restrict access and make firefighting even more difficult.

Indeed, under the guise of being a conservationist, President Obama has been taking lands all over America to keep those lands from being developed for our energy resources of oil, gas, coal, all types of mining -- and any kind of commercial development.

Likewise, President Obama refuses to approve the Keystone oil pipeline from Canada. Worse, in addition to denying America more jobs, Mr. Obama's intention is to eliminate coal, oil and gas in favor of more expensive and unreliable renewable energy.

That's simply the tyranny of using his ideology of big government and the abuse of power against Capitalism free markets and the economy -- plus the abdication of his duty to our national security -- contrary to the best interests and safety of the people. Alas, 2016 can't come too soon.

San Bernardino Sun
October 9, 2014

With plastic bag ban, the state chases fool's gold

Re: "California becomes first state to ban single-use plastic bags" (Sept. 30).

Governor Brown and the Democrat Legislature have done it again. California is now the first in the nation to have a statewide ban on single-use plastic bags, which is another capitulation to extreme environmentalists and an insane inconvenience to grocery shoppers.

Indeed, it will cost businesses and many jobs, which simply adds to the cost of living fraud of AB 32 carbon cap and tax, fuel and oil tax increases, and Brown's costly Proposition 30 tax, and high speed rail deceit. Alas, Democrats' liberal ilk have turned California's gold into fool's gold.

Clearly, with all the businesses and jobs fleeing the state, the only growth going on in California is government, of which we must have freedom from too much destructive ideology, incompetence, taxes, rules, regulations, waste, fraud, lies, deceit and abuse of power. It's simply become an unconstitutional, unconscionable disgrace and must be turned around to constitutional limited government -- no more than we absolutely need. Surely, voters must make the changes we need to survive, thrive and prosper.

VV Daily Press
October 6, 2014

Communicable disease

Allowing illegal aliens and the Ebola disease to come to America is bad enough. Worse, President Obama has the ideological disease that infected his administration, his domestic policy and his foreign policy with incompetence, distraction, lies and deceit.

The question is: how much more damage will the Obama disease cause throughout the remainder of his term, and will it be fatal to our economy and national security? Considering his dismal record, the outlook is bleak at best.

Indeed, Gov. Brown and the Democrat-controlled Legislature and extreme environmentalists are infected with the same ideological disease, which infected California with punishing taxes and regulations against the people, driving up the cost of living and doing business.

Alas, California welcomes illegal aliens and criminals to the state to prey on our taxes, public services, citizens and our property. The only cure for the state and national diseases is our votes. We must use them to survive and prosper.

San Diego Union-Tribune
October 4, 2014

Eric Holder leaves a disgraceful legacy

Attorney General Eric Holder is resigning with a legacy of politics rife with corrupting the office. Indeed, he is intentionally leaving all his unresolved scandals behind. And his racial record has been divisive by design.

Holder is a disgrace to the AG's office and his legacy will undoubtedly be even more revealing, such as persecuting major banks, JP Morgan Chase, the Bank of America and others with heavy fines as punishment for the 2008 housing and financial crash -- when he should have gone after former President Clinton, attorney general

Janet Reno and HUD director Andrew Cuomo for causing the crash by intimidating those banks and others to make home loans to unqualified buyers.

Regardless, Holder had the president's full support as America continues to suffer from the Obama administration's unconscionable legacy of justice lost.

San Diego Union-Tribune
September 18, 2014

Obama lays out case for U.S. involvement

President Obama's speech on his strategy to stop ISIS did little or nothing to excuse his record of failures that allowed the build-up of ISIS into a clear and present danger to America. At this point there is no strategy by the president that will prevent an emboldened ISIS -- with terrorist members from America -- from conducting terrorist attacks against our homeland.

Unfortunately, it is President Obama's dereliction of duty that is the greatest threat to our national security. Indeed, a "God bless the United States of America" won't absolve him of that.

Riverside Press Enterprise
September 16, 2014

Obama's unsure strategies

President Obama's speech on his strategy to stop ISIS did little or nothing to excuse his record of failures that allowed the build-up of ISIS into a clear and present danger to America.

At this point there is no strategy by the president that will prevent an emboldened ISIS -- with terrorist members from America -- from conducting terrorist attacks against our homeland, which, thankfully, did not come on the anniversary of 9/11. Unfortunately, it is President

Obama's dereliction of duty that is the greatest threat to our national security.

Indeed, a "God bless the United States of America" won't absolve him of that.

The O'Reilly Factor
September 11, 2014

Factor Mail - Viewers sound off

"Bill, excellent talking points about protecting the folks from terrorism.

Unfortunately, I believe the President is the greatest threat to national security."

Dan Jeffs
Apple Valley, CA

San Bernardino Sun
September 12, 2014

President Obama's dereliction of duty

President Obama's speech on his strategy to stop ISIS did little or nothing to excuse his record of failures that allowed the build-up of ISIS into a clear and present danger to America.

At this point there is no strategy by the president that will prevent an emboldened ISIS -- with terrorist members from America -- from conducting terrorist attacks against our homeland,

Unfortunately, it is President Obama's dereliction of duty that is the greatest threat to our national security.

Indeed, a "God bless the United States of America" won't absolve him of that.

Los Angeles Times
September 12, 2014

Obama's speech did little to nothing to excuse his record of failures that allowed the buildup of Islamic State into a clear and present danger to America. At this point there is no strategy by the president that will prevent an emboldened Islamic State -- with terrorist members from America -- from conducting terrorist attacks against our homeland,

Unfortunately, it is President Obama's lack of a good strategy to fight the Islamic State that is the greatest threat to our national security. Indeed, a "God bless the United States of America" won't absolve him of that.

The Washington Times
September 1, 2014

Stop the bleeding in California

California's Democrat Legislature pumping out more bills, including a vote to strike Proposition 187, denying state services to illegal aliens from the books, comes as no surprise. Illegals are costing taxpayers $5 to 6 billion, and President Obama's stunt of inviting illegals to cross the border and spreading these people around the country simply adds insult to injury. Alas, at least the good citizens of Murrieta stood up for themselves with some success, and their example should be continued throughout the state.

Indeed, California is steeped in decline from a Democrat Legislature buckling to activist courts, extreme liberals, radical environmentalists; anti-business taxes and onerous regulations. As if that weren't enough, California is also plagued with a failing public education system exacerbated by the selfish interests power of teacher unions, a failed penal system putting the population at extreme risk, punishing taxes on the people and their property and a deceitful, tyrannical government bent on crashing the state.

Hopefully, California voters will wise-up to the fraud and stop the bleeding. Otherwise, California will certainly be headed for voter-assisted social, political and economic suicide....

San Bernardino Sun
August 26, 2014

Why Hillary Clinton should not be the next president

Hillary Clinton and President Obama are painful examples of politicians who blatantly lie to the majority of voters to get elected, then revert to their core ideology to govern.

Clinton was inept as Secretary of State and would do little to nothing to resolve President Obama's foreign policy disaster. Particularly, when she simply did Obama's bidding, pushed the "reset button" with Russia, and exacerbated matters in Libya when she mishandled the Benghazi terrorist attack, costing the lives of four Americans, including our ambassador Chris Stevens.

Clinton's feigned criticism of the president's foreign policy is hypocritically political at the height of the ISIS national security crisis in Iraq.

Hillary Clinton for president? No.

Mike Huckabee for president? Yes.

VV Daily Press
August 25, 2014

Phony Charges

Three-term Governor Rick Perry has performed extremely well as governor of Texas, particularly in his last term in the areas of economic growth, employment, low taxes and carrying on the fight against President Obama's failed border security and immigration policies resulting in the costly flood of illegal immigrant children and families surrendering themselves at the border.

So, how do vindictive Austin Texas Democrats react to Perry's success for all Texans and his potential for another run at the presidency? Travis County officials drum-up phony charges against Governor Perry and indict him with two counts of felony abuse of power after Travis County district attorney, Rosemary Lehmberg refused Perry's demand that she resign after a bitter drunk-driving arrest and conviction -- then vetoed funding for Lehmberg's public integrity unit.

Worse, all of this smacks of President Obama's partisan IRS-style hit-squad against Governor Perry for embarrassing Obama with his tough border security and illegal immigration stand -- and Perry's economic success compared to Obama's economic failures. Indeed, President Obama and Travis County officials are the ones who should be charged with abuse of power to diminish Perry's chances in the 2016 presidential election.

USA TODAY
August 22, 2014

Ferguson shooting

There has been an overreaction and a rush to judgment in the police shooting death of Michael Brown in Missouri, exacerbated by outside hateful activists, looting, violence, President Obama and Attorney General Eric Holder.

Indeed, at this point evidence may lead to the conclusion that the shooting was justified. Unfortunately, it is doubtful that true justice will prevail. [Clearly, this unnecessary situation is a sad commentary on selfish political interests and the decline of our society.]

The Washington Times
August 18, 2014

Perry indictment is an abuse of power

Texas Gov. Rick Perry has performed extremely well in his current position, particularly in his last term, in the areas of economic growth, employment, low taxes and carrying on the fight against President Obama's failed border security and immigration policies. These policies have resulted in the costly flood of illegal-immigrant children and families surrendering themselves at the border.

How do vindictive Austin Texas Democrats react to Perry's success for all Texans and his potential for another run at the presidency? Travis County officials drum-up phony charges against Mr. Perry and indict him with two counts of felony abuse of power after the county district attorney, Rosemary Lehmberg refused Mr. Perry's demand that she resign following a bitter drunken-driving arrest and conviction. Mr. Perry then vetoed funding for Lehmberg's public integrity unit.

Worse, all of this smacks of President Obama's partisan IRS-style hit-squad against Mr. Perry for embarrassing Mr. Obama with his tough border security and illegal immigration stand -- and Mr. Perry's economic success, compared to Mr. Obama's economic failures. Indeed, Mr. Obama and Travis County officials are the ones who should be charged with abuse of power, as they are trying desperately to diminish Mr. Perry's chances in the 2016 presidential election.

The Washington Times
August 15, 2014

No to Hillary in 2016

Hillary Clinton and President Obama are painful examples of politicians who blatantly lie to the majority of voters to get elected, then revert to their core ideology to govern.

Mrs. Clinton was inept as secretary of state and would do little to nothing to resolve President Obama's foreign-policy disaster. Particularly, when she simply did Obama's bidding by pushing the "reset button" with Russia, and exacerbated matters in Libya when she mishandled the Benghazi terrorist attack that cost the lives of four Americans, including our ambassador.

Mrs. Clinton's recent feigned criticism of the president's foreign policy is hypocritically political at the height of the Islamic State crisis in Iraq. If elected president, Mrs. Clinton would still embrace Obamacare as evidenced by her failed attempt at national health care during the Clinton administration.

Hillary Clinton for president? No.

A Republican Congress and Mike Huckabee for president? Yes.

San Diego Union-Tribune
August 13, 2014

Voters must stand up for the nation

Republicans don't hate President Obama. They hate what he is doing to the country, and not for the country.

President Obama has made it painfully clear that from the time he was elected, he was going to fundamentally transform America by whatever means necessary to fit his agenda.

And that's exactly what he has done. First with a Democrat Congress, then with Senate Majority Harry Reid changing the rules and rendering the Republican House powerless, so Obama can govern by executive order and he won't have to veto Republican legislation. Checkmate!

Obama Democrats, lies, diversion, deceit, government growth, abuse of executive power and all. Question is: Will voters lay back and take the indoctrination and loss of freedom, or stand up and take back their government at the ballot box?

San Bernardino Sun
August 8, 2014

Disgraceful leadership fails national security

Commander-in-Chief Obama was in Africa promoting business and aid when Major General Harold J. Greene was assassinated by an Afghan soldier, who shot the general four times in the back.

President Obama said nothing about it -- or the young girls held hostage by African terrorists -- and is just getting around to informally questioning deserter and traitor Sgt. Bergdahl who was traded for 5 major terrorists from GITMO.

Alas, it all amounts to a Dereliction of duty, incompetence and -- coupled with terrorism gone wild in the Ukraine, Iraq, Libya and Israel, and failure in deterring Iran's terrorist state and nuclear weapon ambitions -- a leaderless disgrace of American foreign policy and national security weakness.

VV Daily Press
August 4, 2014

Painfully clear

Republicans don't hate President Obama. They hate what he is doing to the country, and not for the country. President Obama has made it painfully clear that from the time he was elected, he was going to fundamentally transform America by whatever means necessary to fit his agenda.

And that's exactly what he has done. First with a Democrat Congress, then with Senate Majority Harry Reid changing the rules and rendering the Republican House powerless, so Obama can govern by executive order and he won't have to veto Republican legislation. Check mate!

Obama Democrats, lies, diversion, deceit, government growth, abuse of executive power and all.... Question is: will voters lay back and take the indoctrination and loss of freedom, or stand up and take back their government at the ballot box?

Newsmax
August 2014 issue

Prisoner swap probe

As long as Obama is president, it is unlikely Sgt. Bowe Bergdahl will be convicted of anything or even court-martialed ("Hostage swap might signal Gitmo closing." July)

Daniel B. Jeffs
Apple Valley, Calif.

(original letter)

As long as Obama is President, it is unlikely that Sergeant Bergdahl will be convicted of anything or even court-martialed, when in all likelihood, he should be prosecuted for desertion, collaborating with the enemy and treason. The reason is simple. It would make President Obama look even more foolish because of the dangerous trade for five high level Taliban terrorists -- national security be damned.

USA TODAY
July 23, 2014

Is there a choice but to continue Iran talks?

Negotiating with Iran to stop its nuclear weapon development is an exercise in futility. Iran will continue to pursue nuclear weapons until stopped by complete sanctions and military action if necessary.

President Obama's drive to have a nuclear weapon-free world is delusional. Agreeing to reduce our nuclear weapons from about 5000 to 1500 was a deadly mistake, and he wants to reduce them further.

We must retain the deterrent with overwhelming nuclear strength. America is now much more vulnerable and the world is less safe.

San Diego Union-Tribune
July 18, 2014

Californians want the death penalty

The State of California's de facto abolition of the death penalty comes as no surprise, even though the voters of California have made it clear that they want the death penalty.

Judge Cormac J. Carney was correct in ruling that California's execution system of extraordinary delays render the death penalty unpredictable, arbitrary and useless as retribution or deterrent -- thus in violation of the 8th Amendment's prohibition of cruel and unusual punishment.

It's bad enough that a Northern California federal judge incorrectly ruled that California's lethal injection system was cruel and unusual punishment even though it is used in many states and is the most humane way of administering the death penalty.

As a Southern Californian retired from 41 years working in the criminal justice system, I've witnessed California's unconscionable decline in the administration of justice, unnecessarily making the people much less safe and secure against violent crime. That's injustice!

It is well known and understood that the death penalty is a deterrent against murder. California should follow the State of Texas in their administration of the death penalty: After a reasonable time for appeals, the death penalty is carried out as it should be. That's justice!

Daniel B. Jeffs
Carlsbad

(original letter)

The Los Angeles Times -- a federal judge ruling lethal injection unconstitutional -- and the State of California's de facto abolition of the death penalty comes as no surprise, even though the voters of California have made it clear that they want the death penalty.

Orange County Federal judge Cormac J. Carney was correct in ruling that California's execution system of extraordinary delays render the death penalty unpredictable, arbitrary and useless as retribution or deterrent -- thus in violation of the 8th Amendment's prohibition of cruel and unusual punishment.

It's bad enough that a Northern California federal judge incorrectly ruled that California's lethal injection system was cruel and unusual punishment even though it is used in many states and is the most humane way of administering the death penalty.

Surely, the will of the people should prevail regarding the death penalty, not the will of un-American Civil Liberties Union and others who could care less about the victims and families of horrendous murders who should be put to death.

As a Southern Californian retired from 41 years working in the criminal justice system, I've witnessed California's unconscionable decline in the administration of justice, unnecessarily making the people much less safe and secure against violent crime. That's injustice!

It is well known and understood that the death penalty is a deterrent against murder. California should follow the State of Texas in their administration of the death penalty: after a reasonable time for appeals, the death penalty is carried out as it should be. That's justice!

VV Daily Press
July 18, 2014

Militarize the border

It's bad enough that decades of weak border enforcement and weak illegal alien enforcement have imposed too great a burden on American citizens' tax dollars supporting millions of illegal aliens' housing, health care, education and welfare. Indeed, Illegal alien criminals, drug cartel operatives and gangs who prey on our citizens must be stopped along with the out-of-control flow of illegals.

Considering President Obama's refusal to enforce immigration laws and border security, the only solution to stopping unabated border crossings is to militarize the border. That should be done immediately and it should remain that way permanently to keep out criminals, drug cartels, terrorists and the flow of illegal aliens. The security of the American people demands it.

Orange County Register
July 13, 2014
(lead letter of 5 letters)

Obama fails to protect border

President Barack Obama has begun his transformation of America and abdicated his responsibility to enforce laws that do not fit his agenda. Indeed, his intentional failures have turned into a crisis of illegal aliens flowing across the border, including many children from South America -- 100,000 and counting -- most of whom will not be deported.

Worse, President Obama has seriously violated our country's sovereignty, our economy and our domestic and national security by allowing potential terrorists to cross the border. Obama's failed foreign policy is stimulating the proliferation of terrorists in the Middle East who are dedicated to the destruction of America with no remorse.

Coupled with the steady growth of already big government, over-reaching regulations, punishing taxation, and the loss of freedoms, the administration and liberal Democrats' abuse of power are a clear and present danger to our country and American citizens. This can only be overcome by changing the executive, legislative and judicial branches of our government to constitutional limited government -- with our votes. It's a matter of our survival.

VV Daily Press
July 10, 2014

With no remorse

Since he took office, President Obama began his transformation of America and abdicated his responsibility to enforce laws that do not fit his agenda including immigrations laws and the protection of our southern border. Indeed, his intentional failures have turned into a crisis of illegal aliens flowing across the border, including many children from South America -- 100,000 and counting -- most of whom will not be deported.

It's bad enough that there are already about 12 million illegal immigrants in the United States, who are a heavy drain on the states and taxpayers required to provide them with health care, housing, welfare and education. President Obama has purposely exacerbated the problem with open border invitations for millions more, as if North America and South America were one.

Worse, President Obama has seriously violated our country's sovereignty, our economy and our domestic and national security -- by allowing mass illegal immigration, including potential terrorists, criminals and drugs to cross the border -- plus his failed foreign policy stimulating the proliferation of fanatical terrorists in the Middle East who are dedicated to the destruction of America -- with no remorse.

Alas, coupled with the steady growth of already big government, overreaching regulations, punishing taxation, and the loss of freedoms, President Obama, his administration and liberal Democrats' abuse of power are a clear and present danger to our country and American citizens, which can only be overcome by changing the executive, legislative and judicial branches of our government to constitutional limited government -- with our votes. It's a matter of our survival.

San Bernardino Sun
July 10, 2014

Obama abdicates duty to protect border

Since he took office, President Obama began his transformation of America and abdicated his responsibility to enforce laws that do not fit his agenda including immigrations laws and the protection of our southern border. Indeed, his intentional failures have turned into a crisis of illegal aliens flowing across the border, including many children from South America -- 100,000 and counting -- most of whom will not be deported.

It's bad enough that there are already about 12 million illegal immigrants in the United States, who are a heavy drain on the states and taxpayers required to provide them with health care, housing, welfare and education. President Obama has purposely exacerbated the problem with open border invitations for millions more, as if North America and South America were one.

Worse, President Obama has seriously violated our country's sovereignty, our economy and our domestic and national security -- by allowing mass illegal immigration, including potential terrorists, criminals and drugs to cross the border -- plus his failed foreign policy stimulating the proliferation of fanatical terrorists in the Middle East who are dedicated to the destruction of America -- with no remorse.

Alas, coupled with the steady growth of already big government, overreaching regulations, punishing taxation, and the loss of freedoms, President Obama, his administration and liberal Democrats' abuse of power are a clear and present danger to our country and American citizens, which can only be overcome by changing the executive, legislative and judicial branches of our government to constitutional limited government -- with our votes. It's a matter of our survival.

Los Angeles Times
Opinion L.A.
July 9, 2014

President Obama abdicates duty to protect border

Since he took office, President Obama began his transformation of America and abdicated his responsibility to enforce laws that do not fit his agenda including immigrations laws and the protection of our southern border. Indeed, his intentional failures have turned into a crisis of illegal aliens flowing across the border, including many children from South America -- 100,000 and counting -- most of whom will not be deported.

It's bad enough that there are already about 12 million illegal immigrants in the United States, who are a heavy drain on the states and taxpayers required to provide them with health care, housing, welfare and education. President Obama has purposely exacerbated the problem with open border invitations for millions more, as if North America and South America were one.

Worse, President Obama has seriously violated our country's sovereignty, our economy and our domestic and national security -- by allowing mass illegal immigration, including potential terrorists, criminals and drugs to cross the border -- plus his failed foreign policy stimulating the proliferation of fanatical terrorists in the Middle East who are dedicated to the destruction of America -- with no remorse.

Alas, coupled with the steady growth of already big government, overreaching regulations, punishing taxation, and the loss of freedoms, President Obama, his administration and liberal Democrats' abuse of power are a clear and present danger to our country and American citizens, which can only be overcome by changing the executive, legislative and judicial branches of our government to constitutional limited government -- with our votes. It's a matter of our survival.

San Diego Union-Tribune
July 8, 2014

Time to declare our independence again

This 4th of July serves as a painful reminder of what led to declaring our independence from imperial England. Of course, we celebrate the patriotism and meaning of Independence Day, and we are grateful for the history of freedom and liberty that it embodies.

However, as a proud patriotic American, it's sad for me to say that President Obama's imperial presidency has become a promised fundamental transformation of America into a rapidly expanding government of overreaching regulations, taxation, intrusion -- social, political and economic aggression -- and an overall loss of freedoms.

Indeed, President Obama and his administration are out-of-control, making it necessary to declare our independence again -- with our votes -- before it's too late.

VV Daily Press
June 20, 2014

Obama campaigns while al-Qaida burns Iraq

President Obama preaches about global warming to the UC Irvine graduating class -- attends a Democrat fundraiser in Laguna Beach, and vacations in Palm Springs on Father's Day without his children -- while al-Qaida increases its burning invasion of Iraq and continues to grow throughout the Middle East.

Indeed, as al-Qaida drives to combine Syria and Iraq by creating an extreme Islamic state -- to conduct terrorism against America and the West -- Iran is backing Iraq with its military to resist the takeover.

Worse, President Obama's worthless diplomacy -- ignoring the meltdown of the Middle East, and the rapid growth of al-Qaida -- threatens our national security directly, while Iran increases its efforts to develop nuclear weapons, unabated.

LETTERS TO THE EDITOR

Surely, the president must immediately use our airpower to stop and destroy al-Qaida with fighters, missiles, drones and B-2 bombers -- the assistance of the Arab-League. Further dereliction of presidential duty is simply unacceptable.

San Bernardino Sun
June 19, 2014

Obama's policies breaking America's back

With 50,000 unsupervised minor children from Latin America streaming over the border in the past 8 months, it's becoming painfully obvious the President Obama is selling out the nation to illegal immigrants -- asking for $2 billion to take care of them.

Coupled with Obama's intentional policy of nearly open borders, refusal to enforce immigration laws -- and the invitation for illegals to drain hundreds of billions of American citizen's tax dollars for education, healthcare, welfare, housing, and food stamps -- the threat to the nation's stability is being severely undermined.

Worse, If this is allowed to go on unabated, exacerbated by dumping illegal children on Arizona and California's insane open-door policy for illegals, President Obama's failed social, political and economic policies on illegal immigration -- plus his dangerous attacks against U.S. energy and lack of foreign policy causing the Middle East to explode with Islamic terrorist aggression cutting off oil imports from Iraq and elsewhere, which is raising our oil prices -- Obama could very well break America's back by the time he leaves office.

Daily Press
June 16, 2014

President Obama breaking America's back

With 50,000 unsupervised minor children from Latin America streaming over the border in the past 8 months, it's becoming painfully

obvious the President Obama is selling out the nation to illegal immigrants -- asking for $2 billion to take care of them. Coupled with
Obama's intentional policy of nearly open borders, refusal to enforce
immigration laws -- and the invitation for illegals to drain hundreds
of billions of American citizen's tax dollars for education, healthcare,
welfare, housing, and food stamps -- the threat to the nation's stability is being severely undermined. Particularly with the escalation of
illegal alien criminals invading America and preying on our people.

Worse, If this is allowed to go on unabated, exacerbated by dumping illegal children on Arizona and California's insane open-door policy for illegals, President Obama's failed social, political and economic
policies on illegal immigration -- plus his dangerous attacks against
U.S. energy and lack of foreign policy causing the Middle East to
explode with Islamic terrorist aggression cutting off oil imports from
Iraq and elsewhere, which is raising our oil prices -- Obama could very
well break America's back by the time he leaves office.

Daily Press - Dispatch
June 15, 2014
(unedited)

Striking down tenure law sends huge message

Los Angeles Superior Court Judge Rolf M. Treu demonstrated courageous justice in ruling that California teacher tenure is unconstitutional and detrimental to students. Indeed, the setback to California
teacher unions is long overdue, particularly when teachers acquire
tenure after a mere 18 months on the job, thus protecting them
regardless of their competence or job or law violations -- for life.

Tenure was meant for high-level university and college professors who earned it, not summarily granted to every teacher in the
state. Teacher union power, buying politicians, jerking around taxpayers and stealing students' education has gone on far too long.
California's corrupt union establishment of tenure and miseducation
is simply a costly disgrace and a crime against society -- certainly
unconstitutional.

San Diego Union-Tribune
June 11, 2014

Tenure decision: It's about time

Terminate teacher tenure
Los Angeles Superior Court Judge Rolf M. Treu demonstrated courage in ruling that California teacher tenure is unconstitutional and detrimental to students.

Indeed, the setback to California teacher unions is long overdue, particularly when teachers acquire tenure after a mere 18 months on the job, thus protecting them regardless of their competence or job or law violations.

Tenure was meant for high-level university and college professors who earned it, not summarily granted to every teacher in the state. Teacher union power has gone on far too long.

Daniel B. Jeffs
Carlsbad

(original letter)

Terminate teacher tenure

Los Angeles Superior Court Judge Rolf M. Treu demonstrated courageous justice in ruling that California teacher tenure is unconstitutional and detrimental to students. Indeed, the setback to California teacher unions is long overdue, particularly when teachers acquire tenure after a mere 18 months on the job, thus protecting them regardless of their competence or job or law violations -- for life.

Tenure was meant for high-level university and college professors who earned it, not summarily granted to every teacher in the state. Teacher union power, buying politicians, jerking around taxpayers and stealing students' education has gone on far too long. California's corrupt union establishment of tenure and miseducation is simply a costly disgrace and a crime against society -- certainly unconstitutional.

San Diego Union-Tribune
June 7, 2014

Letters to the editor regarding Sgt. Bowe Bergdahl

As long as Obama is President, it is unlikely that Sergeant Bergdahl will be convicted of anything or even court marshaled, when in all likelihood, he should be prosecuted for desertion, collaborating with the enemy and treason. The reason is simple. It would make President Obama look even more foolish because of the dangerous trade for five high level Taliban terrorists -- national security be damned.

San Diego Union-Tribune
May 28, 2014

Elliot Rodger: product of failed society

Elliot Rodger's rampage in Isla Vista, California is the result of bullying, irresponsible parenting, weak 5150 enforcement, corrosive social media, political blindness, and a failed mental health system replete with the hollow interests of psychologists. Indeed, Isla Vista has been needlessly added to the mental illness tragedies of Columbine, Virginia Tech., Sandy Hook, Aurora and others.

Alas, too much of our culture has sunken into a superficial society of selfish interests, social aggression, political tyranny and extremes. Now retired from a 41-year career in law enforcement and the criminal justice system since 1960, I have witnessed the deterioration of society first hand, and I am worried about the future of my children, grandchildren and all American families.

One thing is certain: demonizing Republicans and the NRA is a shallow exercise in futility, particularly when big government built by liberal Democrats and the dangerous indoctrination of students by the education establishment are responsible for our failing society. Indeed, guns don't kill people. People kill people is not a hackneyed phrase. It is the sad truth.

San Bernardino Sun
May 29, 2014

Elliot Rodger is a product of our failed society

Elliot Rodger's rampage in Isla Vista, California is the result of bullying, irresponsible parenting, weak 5150 enforcement, corrosive social media, political blindness, and a failed mental health system replete with the hollow interests of psychologists.

Indeed, Isla Vista has been needlessly added to the mental illness tragedies of Columbine, Virginia Tech., Sandy Hook, Aurora and others.

Alas, too much of our culture has sunken into a superficial society of selfish interests, social aggression, political tyranny and extremes. Now retired from a 41-year career in law enforcement and the criminal justice system since 1960, I have witnessed the deterioration of society first hand, and I am worried about the future of my children, grandchildren and all American families.

One thing is certain: demonizing Republicans and the NRA is a shallow exercise in futility, particularly when big government built by liberal Democrats and the dangerous indoctrination of students by the education establishment are responsible for our failing society. Indeed, guns don't kill people. People kill people is not a hackneyed phrase. It is the sad truth.

San Bernardino Sun
May 23, 2014

Obama to repeat Clinton's disaster

President Obama, newly appointed Fannie-Freddie regulator Mel Watt, HUD Secretary Donovan, Treasury Secretary Lew, Federal Reserve Chairwoman, Yellen and the Dodd-Frank Finance laws are in the process of creating a repeat of the 2007/2008 housing and finance crash -- created by President Clinton, HUD director Andrew Cuomo and Attorney General Janet Reno's forced lowering of home-lending standards for unqualified buyers in their insane drive for affordable housing.

Clearly, President Obama's move to repeat the Clinton disaster to recover the foundering housing market is surely the insanity of repeating the cause of the collapse hoping for a different result.

Instead, Obama's blind ambition for his legacy will surely result in hastening the reality of the looming economic bubble to burst prematurely, causing tidal waves of economic misery and pain.

Alas, President Obama's flagrant abuses of executive power are certainly on track to "fundamentally transform" the social, political and economic core of America into a runaway train wreck causing the demise of liberty, prosperity and our republic of freedom.

Our only hope is for a fundamental transformation of Congress and the Presidency in the 2014 and 2016 elections.

The Washington Times
May 22, 2014

U.S. now a symbol of weakness

The breaking off of talks between Israel and the Palestinians highlights President Obama's failures in foreign policy and national security matters on every front: Iran, Syria, Iraq, the overall Middle East, Afghanistan, Russia, Asia and Europe.

Mr. Obama's continued agenda against our economy, as well as his way of dealing with alien criminals, illegal immigrants and the flow of illegal aliens across our borders, are all seriously damaging our domestic security.

It's simply inexcusable that the United States now stands as the image of weakness in the World. Our economic and national insecurity are evidence of that. Surely, our survival rests with major changes in overreaching government and government leadership, which must be addressed in the 2014 and 2016 elections.

The Washington Times
May 15, 2014

Hypocritical Benghazi panel complaints

House Democrats' complaints over their lack of representation on the Benghazi special committee show fecklessness. With seven Republicans and five Democrats, the committee is simply a fair representation of the percentages of Republicans and Democrats in the House. Indeed, Democrats have falsely branded the select committee a "witch hunt" and made childish threats to either boycott the committee or select only one representative.

Clearly, this is nothing but hypocritical behavior, particularly when it was the Democrat-controlled House and Senate who rammed through Obamacare from behind closed doors with no debate or Republican participation. Of course when passed, President Obama's scheme was quickly signed with his economic poison pen -- followed by the passing and signing of excessive finance laws and economy-busting regulations.

Alas, coupled with the Democrat-controlled Senate stopping all Republican legislation, the malfeasance of the Obama administration's Fast and Furious gun-running scandal, the IRS' targeting of conservative organizations and donors, and Mr. Obama's various energy edicts, there is a clear and present danger to our freedoms and security.

Certainly, California is a glaring example of the damage Democrat-dominated governments can do to our society. The current government must be changed in the 2014 and 2016 elections -- for America's survival.

Daniel B. Jeffs
Apple Valley, Calif.

(original letter)

House Democrats' feckless complaints over their lack of representation on the Benghazi disaster select committee with 7 Republicans and 5 Democrats is simply a fair representation of the percentages of Republicans and Democrats in the House. Indeed, Democrats have falsely branded the select committee a "Witch Hunt" and made childish threats to either boycott the committee or select only one representative.

Clearly, this is nothing but scurrilous hypocritical behavior, particularly when it was the Democrat-controlled House and Senate who rammed through Obamacare from behind closed doors with no debate or Republican participation. Of course when passed, President Obama's Affordable Care Act was quickly signed with his economic poison pen -- followed by passing and signing tyrannical finance laws and economy-busting regulations.

Alas, coupled with the Democrat Senate stopping all Republican legislation, the malfeasance of the Obama administration's "Fast and Furious," the IRS targeting of conservative organizations and donors -- plus presidential EPA and energy edicts and other flagrant abuse of power executive orders trampling democracy, justice, our republic and the Constitution by circumventing Congress -- surely, along with seriously weakened foreign policy and national security -- there is a clear and present danger to our freedoms and security.

Certainly, California is a glaring example of what Democrat-dominated damage has done and is doing to our society, all of which means that our socialist government, education establishment, and complicit media's reckless direction must be changed in the 2014 and 2016 elections -- for America's survival.

USA TODAY
May 2, 2014

Stalled Mideast talks reflect weak Obama administration

The break-off of talks between Israel and Palestine highlights President Obama's failures in foreign policy and national security matters on every front: Iran, Syria, Iraq, the overall Middle East, Afghanistan, Russia, Asia and Europe.

It's simply inexcusable that the United States now stands as the image of weakness in the World, and with it, our economic and national insecurity. Surely, our survival rests with major changes in overreaching government and government leadership, which must be addressed in the 2014 and 2016 elections.

Daniel B. Jeffs
Apple Valley, Calif.

(Original letter)

The break-off of talks between Israel and Palestine highlights President Obama's failures in foreign policy and national security matters on every front: Iran, Syria, Iraq, the overall Middle East, Afghanistan, Russia, Asia and Europe.

Of course Mr. Obama's continued agenda against our economy, and in dealing with alien criminals, illegal immigrants and the flow of illegal aliens across our borders is seriously damaging our domestic security.

It's simply inexcusable that the United States now stands as the image of weakness in the World, and with it, our economic and national insecurity. Surely, our survival rests with major changes in over-reaching government and government leadership, which must be addressed in the 2014 and 2016 elections.

VV Daily Press
April 29, 2014

Don't blame Pope John Paul II

Pope John Paul II should have explained that the church was infiltrated by pedophile priests who entered Catholic seminaries during the aggressive gay movement of the 70's and 80's.

Indeed, the church was mostly unaware of the unconscionable pedophiles -- who were purposely becoming priests to prey upon the ample supplies of altar boys -- and church leaders struggled too long with it.

Pope Francis would do well for the church by explaining the historical problem openly. Certainly, leaders of the gay community should break their silence and condemn all pedophile priests.

Surely, the Catholic church should not be blamed for their unspeakable sins. And surely, Pope John Paul's sainthood should not be blemished by it.

San Bernardino Sun
April 29, 2014

Turn over land to states

Regarding the Nevada Bundy cattle ranching/grazing case: With the exception of military bases, the federal government should turn over all federal lands to the states for private use, including national forests, parks and monuments. The states and the people would gain from what the federal government has grossly mismanaged.

The Washington Times
April 28, 2014

Pedophile priests' sins aren't church's

Pope John Paul II should have explained that the church was infiltrated by pedophile priests who entered Catholic seminaries during the aggressive homosexual movement of the 1970's and 80's.

Indeed, the church was mostly unaware of the unconscionable pedophiles who were deliberately becoming priests to prey upon the ample supplies of altar boys, and church leaders struggled too long with it.

Pope Francis would do well for the church by explaining the historical problem openly. Certainly, leaders of the homosexual community should break their silence and condemn all pedophile priests. The Catholic Church should not be blamed for pedophiles' unspeakable sins. Surely, Pope John Paul's sainthood should not be blemished by it.

Riverside Press Enterprise
April 23, 2014

Give Bundy fairness

When Nevada had to give up most of its land to the federal government as a condition for statehood, it was wrong. The land should be returned to the state. Clearly, the way Nevada's cattle-ranching Bundy family and their supporters are being intimidated by federal agents is outrageous.

Likewise, Harry Reid, the U.S. Senator from Nevada undoubtedly called out Bureau of Land Management rangers against the Bundy's and their cattle. Indeed, Reid's abuse of power and calling Bundy supporters "domestic terrorists" simply adds fuel to the fire, and it's blatantly un-American.

With the exception of military bases, the federal government should turn over all federal lands to the states for private use, including national forests, parks and monuments. The states and the people could then gain from what the federal government and environmental/conservation zealots have grossly mismanaged.

Daily Press Apple Valley Review
Commentary by Daniel B. Jeffs
April 22, 2014

Medicare Advantage for all

Democrats fighting Obama over Medicare are up for re-election as compared to Democrats who continue to support Obamacare talking points designed to eliminate Medicare Advantage to help pay for the Unaffordable Careless Act. Indeed, president and CEO of America's Health Insurance Plans, Karen Ignagni correctly points out that repeating the 1997 Medicare Advantage cuts would cause more millions of seniors to lose their health care coverage.

My wife and I have been enrolled in Kaiser's Senior Advantage healthcare program since 2006, and for many years I have closely followed government's inept mishandling of Medicare and Medicaid. Kaiser should be the model of excellence in handling the Medicare Advantage program, which if followed, would provide Medicare Advantage to all seniors for less than traditional Medicare.

Of course, it would require government to abandon Obamacare's exacerbated road to ruin, reform both Medicare and the mass expansion of the Medicaid fiasco, and restore common sense to health care. Alas, it would also relieve the costly chaos in the nation's emergency rooms. Rather than causing the American people and our economy to suffer the cost and pain of unaffordable health care, allow the nation's private health care industry to do its job.

Daniel B. Jeffs is an Apple Valley resident and author of the series, "Letters to the Editor:
From the Trenches of Democracy."

VV Daily Press
April 21, 2014

Abuse of power

When Nevada had to give up most of its land to the federal government as a condition for statehood, it was wrong and the land should be returned to the state. Clearly, the way Nevada's cattle-ranching Bundy family and their supporters are being intimidated by federal storm-troopers is outrageous.

Likewise, Nevada Senator Harry Reid undoubtedly called-out BLM Rangers against the Bundy's and their cattle. Indeed, Reid's abuse of power and calling Bundy supporters domestic terrorists simply adds fuel to the fire, and it's blatantly un-American.

With the exception of military bases, the federal government should turn over all federal lands to the states for private use, including national forests, parks and monuments. The states and the people could then gain from what the federal government and environmental/conservation zealots have grossly mismanaged.

(original letter)

When Nevada had to give up most of its land to the federal government as a condition for statehood, it was wrong and the land should be returned to the state. Clearly, the way Nevada's cattle-ranching Bundy family and their supporters are being intimidated by federal storm-troopers is outrageous.

Nevada Senator Harry Reid undoubtedly called-out BLM Rangers against the Bundy's and their cattle. Now he is forming a federal task force to deal with it. Indeed, Reid's abuse of power and calling Bundy supporters domestic terrorists simply adds fuel to the fire, which is blatantly un-American -- tantamount to domestic federal terrorism.

With the exception of military bases, the federal government should turn over all federal lands to the states for private use, including national forests, parks and monuments. The states and the people could then gain from what the federal government and environmental/conservation zealots have grossly mismanaged.

The Washington Times
April 9, 2014

Allow private health care industry to do job

Democrats fighting Obama over Medicare are up for re-election. Democrats who continue to support Obamacare talking points designed to eliminate Medicare Advantage in order to help pay for Obamacare are not.

Indeed, America's Health Insurance Plans CEO Karen Ignagni correctly points out that repeating the 1997 Medicare Advantage cuts would cause millions of seniors to lose their health care coverage.

My wife and I have been enrolled in Kaiser's Senior Advantage healthcare program since 2006, and for many years I have closely followed government's inept mishandling of Medicare and Medicaid. Kaiser should be the model of excellence in handling the Medicare Advantage program, which if followed, would provide Medicare Advantage to all seniors for less than traditional Medicare.

Of course, it would require government to abandon Obamacare's exacerbated road to ruin, reform both Medicare and the mass expansion of the Medicaid fiasco, and restore common sense to health care. Alas, it would also relieve the costly chaos in the nation's emergency rooms.

Rather than causing the American people and our economy to suffer the cost and pain of unaffordable health care, allow the nation's private health care industry to do its job.

Daily Press Apple Valley Review
Commentary by Daniel B. Jeffs
April 8, 2014

The perfect social, political and economic storm

California and America's perfect social, political and economic storm is on the horizon. Indeed, it's bad enough that socialism has taken root with public education indoctrination, environmental zealots have weakened our energy resources, extreme regulation is dragging down our economy.

Adding insult to injury, Hollywood and the media are perpetuating the lies about Wall Street being responsible for the 2008 crash, when it was the Clinton administration that caused the collapse with forced loans to unqualified homebuyers.

Governor Brown, the Democrat legislature, AG Kamala Harris, and the extreme environmental and teacher union lobbies continue to attack California's economy by supporting failed education, the proliferation of illegal aliens, bad prison reform, the costly high speed rail, higher taxes, unreasonable restrictions on energy and water resources -- and refusing to defend voter initiatives, while working to weaken the constitutional rights of the people to ballot measure direct democracy when needed.

Coupled with President Obama and congressional Democrats' abuse of power and unconstitutional attacks on the people, our society and our economy -- with national healthcare, national education, over-regulation, dangerously weak foreign policy and growing threats to our national security -- they have created a perfect storm driven by biased media that is relentlessly rolling across America -- unabated. Surely, our survival depends on major changes in the 2014 and 2016 elections.

Obama's unimpeachable abuse of power

It doesn't matter that the Obama administration has and will be replete with government growth, lies, deceit, diversion, distraction and the wholesale-unconstitutional abuse of power that will dangerously damage our freedoms, our society, our economy, and our national security -- unabated. President Obama will never be impeached and removed from office. Indeed, no matter how you spin it, the unintended consequences of political correctness has been glaringly intended simply because that's what socialism-Marxism is.

Daniel B. Jeffs is an Apple Valley resident and author of the series, "Letters to the Editor:
From the Trenches of Democracy."

San Bernardino Sun
April 2, 2014

The perfect social, political storm

California and America's perfect social, political and economic storm is on the horizon. Indeed, it's bad enough that socialism has taken root with public education indoctrination, environmental zealots have weakened our energy resources, and extreme regulation is dragging down our economy. Adding insult to injury, Hollywood and the media are perpetuating the lies about Wall Street being

responsible for the 2008 crash, when it was the Clinton administration that caused the collapse with forced loans to unqualified
homebuyers.

Gov. Brown, the Democrat legislature, Attorney General Kamala
Harris, and the extreme environmental and teacher union lobbies
continue to attack California's economy by supporting failed education, the proliferation of illegal aliens, bad prison reform, the costly
high speed rail, higher taxes, unreasonable restrictions on energy
and water resources -- and refusing to defend voter initiatives, while
working to weaken the constitutional rights of the people to ballot
measure direct democracy when needed.

Coupled with President Obama and congressional Democrats'
abuse of power and unconstitutional attacks on the people, our society and our economy -- with national healthcare, national education, over-regulation, dangerously weak foreign policy and growing
threats to our national security -- they have created a perfect storm
driven by biased media that is relentlessly rolling across America.
Surely, our survival depends on major changes in the 2014 and 2016
elections.

Los Angeles Times
Opinion L.A.
March 30, 2014

Re: Three senators suspended, and it's a lose-lose-lose for
Californians by Kerry Cavanaugh
March 28, 2014

The perfect social, political and economic storm

California and America's perfect social, political and economic
storm is on the horizon. Indeed, it's bad enough that socialism has
taken root with public education indoctrination, environmental zealots have weakened our energy resources, and extreme regulation is
dragging down our economy. Adding insult to injury, Hollywood
and the media are perpetuating the lies about Wall Street being

responsible for the 2008 crash, when it was the Clinton administration that caused the collapse with forced loans to unqualified homebuyers.

Governor Brown, the Democrat legislature, AG Kamala Harris, and the extreme environmental and teacher union lobbies continue to attack California's economy by supporting failed education, the proliferation of illegal aliens, bad prison reform, the costly high speed rail, higher taxes, unreasonable restrictions on energy and water resources -- and refusing to defend voter initiatives, while working to weaken the constitutional rights of the people to ballot measure direct democracy when needed.

Coupled with President Obama and congressional Democrats' abuse of power and unconstitutional attacks on the people, our society and our economy -- with national healthcare, national education, over-regulation, dangerously weak foreign policy and growing threats to our national security -- they have created a perfect storm driven by biased media that is relentlessly rolling across America -- unabated. Surely, our survival depends on major changes in the 2014 and 2016 elections.

Riverside Press Enterprise
March 23, 2014

Weaken Putin's grip

Sanctions on individuals from Putin's inner circle are weak at best. Particularly, when Putin trades sanctions and says he will respond by not supporting sanctions against Iran.

President Obama can easily deal with Putin's aggression by immediately approving the export of natural gas to Europe, the Keystone pipeline -- and by stopping all U.S. technical assistance in extracting oil and gas from Siberia.

Indeed, Russia's economy is already teetering. Further sanctions against Russian imports, world banking and replacement of missiles carelessly removed from Poland, Turkey and other areas would bring Putin to his knees.

Surely, President Obama's weak foreign policy and dealings with Putin are largely responsible for Putin's aggression and being a feigned peacemaker with Syria and Iran. A Nobel Prize for Putin should be out of the question.

Alas, President Obama's Peace Prize was premature and is far from being earned.

Los Angeles Times
Opinion L.A.
March 22, 2014

Re: Democrat's chances in this Fall's Senate elections just turned a little bleaker by Doyle McManus
March 19, 2014

Senate Democrats in trouble with Medicare Advantage

Leading Senate Democrats, who voted for Obamacare -- and are now opposing the cuts to Medicare Advantage because they are up for re-election -- are little more than pandering political hypocrites who will slice Medicare Advantage the day after their re-election. Senior voters in their states should not buy the snake oil. If they do, they will certainly pay the price of deception with less health care and higher prices.

Clearly, it's no time for making deals with the devils, and the devils know it. Especially, when the flow of Boomers into Medicare will substantially increase Medicare Advantage enrollment. That's the good news for seniors, and the bad news for President Obama and Democrats.

Particularly, when 28% of seniors are enrolled in Medicare Advantage, and one of two people eligible for Medicare chooses Advantage, and enrollment is growing at a 10% annual clip -- simply because government turns control of health care over to private plans that manage Medicare, with more flexible services and benefits than traditional Medicare, and "seamless delivery of health care services," -- for better health care outcomes, and higher quality health care.

My wife and I are enrolled in Kaiser Senior Advantage, which is the leading Medicare Advantage manager and a shining example for other Advantage programs to emulate. Indeed, we received the best of care -- well worth the premiums -- and we firmly believe it should be the standard for all senior health care.

President Bush's Medicare Advantage program was the best thing that happened to Medicare since its inception. Government's failure to reduce and eliminate the vast fraud, waste and abuse in Medicare and Medicaid is bad enough. However, President Obama's early assault on Medicare Advantage -- as a presidential candidate -- plus the forced passage of Obama/Democrat Unaffordable Health Careless Act that attacks Medicare Advantage with forthcoming cuts was unconscionable.

San Bernardino Sun
February 28, 2014

California water crisis is criminal

California's current drought-water crisis has been caused, as usual, by environmental zealots and liberal government who have stolen California's gold and our economy.

Adding insult to injury, federal officials from the Bureau of Reclamation announced that the agricultural Central Valley Project and California Water Project customers will receive no water allocations this year.

Indeed, the California Water Project and the Central Valley Project were created, paid for, and maintained by farmers and property owners to deliver Northern California water to the agricultural-rich Central Valley, and 25 million people in Southern California.

It is simply criminal that environmentalists and an activist federal judge have unconstitutionally interfered with private water contracts and made substantial cuts in water delivery from the Sacramento Delta to protect the tiny Delta Smelt fish since 2007 -- which during this drought has exacerbated the water crisis by allowing 800,000 acre feet of San Joaquin River water per year to flow to the ocean.

Fortunately, perceptive management from our California Water Project contractor, The Mojave Water Agency has indicated that from conservation programs and underground banking and storage of water supplies in our Mojave Desert area, we have more than enough water for three years, regardless of drought conditions.

Daily Press Apple Valley Review
February 25, 2014
Commentary by Daniel B. Jeffs

California water, energy crisis

California's current drought-water crisis and looming energy crisis have been caused, as usual, by environmental zealots and liberal government who have stolen California's gold and our economy.

Indeed, the California Water Project was created, paid for, and maintained by property owners to deliver Northern California water to the agricultural-rich Central Valley, and 25 million people in Southern California.

However, environmentalists and an activist federal judge have unconstitutionally interfered with private water contracts and cut water delivery from the Sacramento Delta to protect the tiny Delta Smelt fish, which during this drought has exacerbated the water crisis. Never mind that over 800,000 acre feet of San Joaquin River water per year is being allowed to flow to the ocean.

The state water department proposed a $25 billion tunnel system to resolve the problem, which has not moved forward, yet the unnecessary $68 to $100 billion high-speed-rail debacle is still in play.

Then comes another natural gas energy crisis. Nothing was learned from the previous crisis, costing Californians $billions in electric and heating bills. Certainly, California's environmental and governmental insanity have caused the economic chaos with punishing regulations, and severely limiting California's rich natural resources of natural gas -- and oil, which could reduce gas and energy prices.

Simply put, California has the resources to be self-sufficient with water, energy and gas, without any imports, which we are far too dependent on, leaving us vulnerable to ideology-caused crisis that endanger all Californians.

Attention: Governor Brown, environmental zealots and the Democrat Legislature. Get out of government so we can survive, thrive and prosper.

Daniel B. Jeffs is an Apple Valley resident and the author of the series, "Letters to the Editor:

From the Trenches of Democracy."

Daily Press
February 24, 2014

Water, water everywhere

California water crisis is criminal

California's current drought-water crisis has been caused, as usual, by environmental zealots and liberal government who have stolen California's gold and our economy.

Adding insult to injury, federal officials from the Bureau of Reclamation announced that the agricultural Central Valley Project and California Water Project customers will receive no water allocations this year.

Indeed, the California Water Project and the Central Valley Project were created, paid for, and maintained by farmers and property owners to deliver Northern California water to the agricultural-rich Central Valley, and 25 million people in Southern California.

It is simply criminal that environmentalists and an activist federal judge have unconstitutionally interfered with private water contracts and made substantial cuts in water delivery from the Sacramento Delta to protect the tiny Delta Smelt fish since 2007 -- which during this drought has exacerbated the water crisis by allowing 800,000 acre feet of San Joaquin River water per year to flow to the ocean.

Fortunately, perceptive management from our California Water Project contractor, The Mojave Water Agency has indicated that from conservation programs and underground banking and storage of water supplies in our Mojave Desert area, we have more than enough water for three years, regardless of drought conditions.

USA TODAY
February 14, 2014

Games out of touch with tradition

When I participated in high school track and field as a cross country runner in the 1950's, my understanding of the Olympics was traditional and related to the original competition. Since then, I have been extremely disappointed in the expansion to include events that have little or nothing to do with the original Olympics.

Adding the Winter Olympics and the multitude of sideshow competitions from modern sports, of which there is already too much, is simply a disgrace to real meaning of the Olympics.

As if that were not bad enough, it was a gross mistake to have the Winter Olympics in Russia -- under the dangerous and miserable circumstances. Also, the broadcast of the games interferes with television programming, which is inconsiderate. Not everyone is interested in the winter games. Indeed, it's time to restore the original Olympics.

San Bernardino Sun
February 13, 2014

Restore the traditional meaning of the Olympics

When I participated in high school track and field as a mile and cross country runner in the 1950's, my motives and understanding of the Olympics was traditional to the original games.

Since then, I have been extremely disappointed decade after decade in the expansion of events from track and field, wrestling and archery -- into events that have little or nothing to do with what the Olympics is supposed to be: the suspension of world tensions and hostilities to gather Olympic athletes from all nations to participate in the friendly competition of the games, which have a positive effect on international relations.

Adding the Winter Olympics and the multitude of side-show competitions from modern sports -- which there is already too much of -- to basket weaving, is simply a disgrace to real meaning of the Olympics.

As if that were not bad enough, it was a gross mistake to have the Winter Olympics in Russia -- under the dangerous and miserable circumstances -- and it's an annoying interference with television programming and quality series, which is simply inconsiderate. [Particularly, when there are probably not that many people interested in the winter games. Indeed, it's time to restore the original Olympics.]

Daily Press Apple Valley Review
February 11, 2014
Commentary by Daniel B. Jeffs

Governor Brown is the California flim-flam man

It was bad enough that Governor Brown lied to voters to get the Proposition 30 tax hikes passed, then used the money to prop up the teachers' retirement fund instead of what it was intended for. That was obvious pay back for supporting his election.

Adding insult to injury, he sucked-in voters to pass a bond measure for his pet project high-speed rail plan, when voters had no idea that it would cost ten or more times the estimate. That was unconscionable.

Worse, Brown spent $250 million from AB-32 cap-and-trade funds -- stolen from businesses -- on his toy train, which were never intended for that purpose, and left the rail project hanging because he could not come up with the $20 billion to qualify for federal funding.

Even worse, when Brown took the maximum campaign contribution for his re-election from his high-speed rail contractor, it was conflict of interest business as usual for California's chief executive, the flim-flam man.

Indeed, his re-election is no longer an option.

What's up, Mr. President?

The Congressional Budget Office report is simply another negative for Obamacare. Middle class taxpayers will be forced to subsidize lower income people's health insurance, and they will also have to pay higher insurance premiums for less coverage.

How fair is that, President Obama? Especially, when you say people should work hard and be responsible to reach the middle class.

How deceptive is that, Mr. President? Your Affordable Care Act (unaffordable careless act) is a contradiction in terms, and will seriously damage our economy and hardworking, responsible people.

Indeed, Mr. President, you are taking America down the socialist road to a government-dependent, giant underclass. Surely -- along with abusing your power with edicts and executive orders, using the IRS against those who oppose you, and your dangerous foreign policy -- that's the ideological idea, isn't it, Mr. President?

Daniel B. Jeffs is an Apple Valley resident and author of the series, "Letters to the Editor:
From the Trenches of Democracy."

Newsmax Magazine
February 2014 issue

Shaky legal ground

President Obama told the lie about people being able to keep their health insurance and doctors so many times, it became the truth to them. Telling the people he meant something different after the lie was exposed doesn't make it any less of a lie.

That lie is costing millions of Americans millions of dollars for canceled insurance and forcing them to buy more costly insurance with less coverage and higher deductibles to meet the requirements of the Affordable Care Act.

Daniel B. Jeffs
Apple Valley, Calif.

(Original letter)

President Obama's big lie

President Obama told the lie about people being able to keep their health insurance and doctors so many times, it became the truth to them. Telling the people he meant something different after the lie was exposed doesn't make it any less of a lie.President Obama told the lie about people being able to keep their health insurance and doctors so many times, it became the truth to them. Telling the people he meant something different after the lie was exposed doesn't make it any less of a lie.

That lie is costing millions of Americans millions of dollars for cancelled insurance and forcing them to buy more costly insurance with less coverage and higher deductibles to meet the requirements of the (Un)Affordable Care Act.

Indeed, that's not only unconstitutional, it's fraudulent and an unconscionable and impeachable offense, period!

Daily Press Apple Valley Review
January 28, 2014
Commentaryby Daniel B. Jeffs

Obamacareless ruining the economy

When presidential candidate, Barack Obama campaigned for national healthcare because people were going bankrupt from medical bills, and lied about people being able to keep the health care plans and doctors, it was preview of his abuse of authority when pushing through the Affordable Care Act.

Indeed, the bad actors in the Democrat-controlled Congress abused their authority when ramming through the Act without debate and behind closed doors, and the Supreme Court Judiciary abdicated their duty to justice with their failure to find the Act unconstitutional.

Worse, the Affordable Care Act is turning into the Unaffordable Obama careless Act destined to ruining the economy with cancelled health insurance, raising the cost of healthcare, bankrupting health insurance companies, increasing costs of businesses, and raising the cost of living for most Americans.

It was bad enough that the Clinton administration created the housing bubble by forcing banks to make home loans to unqualified borrowers to create affordable housing, and caused the housing and finance collapse. Surely, the unaffordable health care act should be knocked down, eliminated, and replaced with reasonable health care reforms as necessary.

Deport Justin Bieber

Justin Bieber's arrest for DUI, unlicensed driving and resisting arrest in Miami is the last straw in the Canadian pop star's bad behavior in America. It's bad enough that Bieber thinks he can do whatever he wants with impunity. But when he races dangerously around the country and constantly terrorizes and assaults his neighbors, he has no place here. Indeed, when this Canadian's act has become that bad, his welcome in America is worn out and he should be deported before he kills someone.

Daniel B. Jeffs is an Apple Valley resident and the author of the series,
"Letters to the Editor:
From the Trenches of Democracy."

USA TODAY
January 16, 2014

Easing sanctions a mistake

President Obama easing sanctions and delaying further sanctions in his six-month agreement with Iran over nuclear inspections is a deal with the devil. Indeed, Iran has a long history of misusing diplomacy to buy time for furthering its devious activities in gaining more power in the region.

Iran's nuclear weapon development is much more dangerous than all of its previous assaults on Israel, and its advancement of power in Iraq, Syria and other Mideast nations. Clearly, a nuclear weapon Iran would work toward the annihilation of Israel.

Easing sanctions on Iran and threatening to veto increased sanctions on Iran by Congress is naïve. Iran's false promise to restrict uranium enrichment and allow inspections will result in Iran developing a nuclear weapon. Israel knows it and will not allow Iran to do it.

All President Obama will accomplish will be an attack on Iran by Israel, the proliferation of war in the region, and increased national and global security threats.

Riverside Press Enterprise
January 15, 2014

Leftism is strangling state

Urging budget restraint, feigning discipline, gunning for re-election and another shot at the presidency, Gov. Brown is continuing his long history of grandstanding as a skilled political con man in rolling out his latest state budget fraud. ("Spending binge" No," Our Views, Jan. 10)

Indeed, Brown's 8.5 percent budget increase to $106.8 billion, laced with promises to pay $11 billion toward old debt and put a paultry $1.6 billion into a "rainy day" fund is nothing in the face of hundreds of billions of dollars in long-term liabilities.

Worse, if Prop. 98 -- which requires a minimum percentage of the state budget be spent on K-12 education -- is not repealed by voter initiative, the bulk of the state budget designated for the miseducation money-pit will continue to grow like a metastasizing cancer, exacerbated by the billions wasted annually on health care, welfare and driver licenses for millions of illegal immigrants.

Joined with the governor's bullet-train debacle, the soon-to-be skyrocketing cap-and-trade electricity rates and activist judges jeopardizing public safety regarding the state prison system, our unconscionable state government is forcing Californians down the pathway to insecurity and poverty.

Daily Press Apple Valley Review
January 14, 2014
COMMENTARY

Governor Brown: Budget con man by Daniel B. Jeffs

Urging budget restraint, feigning discipline, gunning for re-election and another shot at the presidency, Governor Brown is continuing his long history of grandstanding as a skilled political con man and taxpayer snake oil salesman who, along with his Democrat cronies dominating the Legislature -- turning it into a liberal agenda Star Chamber -- is rolling out his latest state budget fraud.

Indeed, Brown's 8.5 percent budget increase to $107 billion is laced with promises to pay $11 billion on long term debt -- and $1.6 billion in chump change designated as a "rainy day" fund with a move to promote a permanent fund with a ballot measure -- is nothing in the face of the teachers' $10.2 billion legal extortion retirement contribution and looming $217.8 billion insolvency of Teachers' Retirement System, already $80 billion in the red.

Worse, if Proposition 98 is not repealed by a voter initiative, the bulk of the state budget designated for the state's miseducation money-pit will continue to grow like a metastasizing cancer, exacerbated by the $6 billion per year being wasted on education, healthcare, welfare and drivers' licenses for millions of illegal immigrants.

Coupled with the governor's Prop.30 tax lies, his pet $68-150 billion bullet-train debacle, and the soon-to-be skyrocketing cap-and-trade electricity rates compromising the economy even further -- plus activist federal judges violating California Water Project contracts and state prison system public safety meddling -- our unconscionable state government is forcing Californians down the pathway to insecurity and taxpayer poverty.

Daniel B. Jeffs is an Apple Valley resident and the author of the series,
"Letters to the Editor:
From the Trenches of Democracy."

San Bernardino Sun
January 2, 2014

Governor Brown for president in 2016?

Those in the media and others who are toying with the idea of California Governor Jerry Brown as a candidate for president in 2016 are promoting a bad joke.

Indeed, Governor Brown opposed Proposition 13 in his former life as governor, refused to defend Proposition 8 when he was attorney general, and during this term as Governor committed several serious political crimes. He lied and suckered voters into phony tax increases with Proposition 30 to prevent a $6 billion cut in education funds, and is instead using the money to prop up teacher pensions. Brown also snookered voters to approve bonds for a high speed rail from San Francisco to L.A. that will cost over ten times the advertised expense.

Worse, the Governor and Legislature have encouraged and supported illegal immigration and approved the impact of over 2 million illegals costing taxpayers over $5 billion per year in education, welfare, housing and health care.

Governor Brown may be the curiosity presidential candidate poster boy for his multiple runs for the office, which is no problem for Californians.

Our voters simply need to dump our political poltergeist in his 2014 run for re-election, elect a Republican governor and change the balance of power in the Legislature, or the golden state will surely complete its transformation into fool's gold and total social, political and economic erosion.

(Original letter - edited for space)

Those in the media and others who are toying with the idea of California Governor Jerry Brown as a candidate for president in 2016 are promoting a bad joke. As a California resident since 1944 -- an Eagle Scout and retired from 41 years in the criminal justice system -- who has followed the rise and fall of a great state, I can attest to the fact that Governor Brown, along with other venomous politicians such as minority leader Nancy Pelosi, Senator Barbara Boxer, the

Democrat Legislature and environmentalist cabal are largely responsible for what is likely to become our demise.

Indeed, Governor Brown opposed Proposition 13 in his former life as governor, refused to defend Proposition 8 when he was attorney general, and during this term as Governor committed several serious political crimes. He lied and suckered voters into phony tax increases with Proposition 30 to prevent a $6 billion cut in education funds, and is instead using the money to prop up teacher pensions. Brown also snookered voters to approve bonds for a high speed rail from San Francisco to L.A. that will cost over ten times the advertised expense.

Worse, the Governor and Legislature have encouraged and supported illegal immigration and approved the impact of over 2 million illegals costing taxpayers over $5 billion per year in education, welfare, housing and health care.

Coupled with the state invasive 2009 federal court order to reduce California's prison population, and the surrender of Democrats 2011 AB 109 prisoner realignment, Governor Brown is releasing thousands of felons early -- who are preying on the people and their neighborhoods -- and he is dumping felony prisoners on local jails resulting on even more releases.

Governor Brown may be the curiosity presidential candidate poster boy for his multiple runs for the office, which is no problem for Californians. Our voters simply need to dump our political poltergeist in his 2014 run for re-election, elect a Republican governor and change the balance of power in the Legislature, or the golden state will surely complete its transformation into fool's gold and total social, political and economic erosion.

VV Daily Press
December 18, 2013

Maintain the embargo

President Obama's friendly behavior with Raul Castro is unconscionable. Communist Castro Cuba is our enemy and still the greatest immediate threat to our homeland, just 90 miles off our coast.

61

Lest we forget, the Cuban/Soviet missile crisis nearly developed into nuclear war. Indeed, Cuba has a history of sending its worst criminals to us and can easily ship terrorists to America.

The embargo against Cuba should stand as long as the Castro family maintains the dictatorship and suppresses freedom.

Riverside Press Enterprise
December 15, 2013

Prioritize patriots

Former South African leader Nelson Mandela's greatness notwithstanding, the press' and President Obama's preference in paying more attention to him than those who died during the attack on Pearl Harbor on December 7, 1941, is unconscionable.

Issuing a Pearl Harbor Remembrance Day Proclamation and laying a wreath is not enough.

Obama should have attended the ceremonies at Pearl Harbor and paid tribute to the victims, survivors and World War II veterans.

The terminal lack of patriotism by Obama and the media is simply shameful.

San Bernardino Sun
December 12, 2013

Pearl Harbor remembrance given short shrift

Mandela's greatness notwithstanding, the news media and President Obama's obsession with his life and a lack of Pearl Harbor media coverage in favor of Mandela is unconscionable.

President Obama's issuing his annual Pearl Harbor Remembrance Day Proclamation and laying a wreath is not enough. Indeed, the terminal lack of patriotism by President Obama and the media is simply shameful.

Daniel B. Jeffs
Apple Valley

(original letter)

Mandela's greatness notwithstanding, the news media and President Obama's obsession with his life -- without a Presidential attendance at Pearl Harbor remembering the December 7th, 1941 attack honoring the victims, survivors and WWII veterans -- and a lack of Pearl Harbor media coverage in favor of Mandela is unconscionable. Issuing his annual December 6th Pearl Harbor Remembrance Day Proclamation and laying a wreath is not enough. Indeed, the terminal lack of patriotism by President Obama and the media is simply shameful.

NewsMax Magazine
December 2013 Issue

ObamaCare's Failings

President Obama targeted the government shutdown, from closing national parks to denying death benefits to families of our military heroes killed in action to inflict as much pain on the public as possible (Employees Dump Workers Onto Private Exchanges," November).

Our country will surely feel the social, political and economic pain of Obamacare, hopefully in time for voters to reject the socialist takeover in the 2014 and 2016 elections.

(Excepts from original letter below)

Government shutdown scam

President Obama targeted the government shutdown -- from closing national parks to denying death benefits to families of our military heroes killed in action -- to inflict as much pain on the public as possible -- and to spread fear over the debt limit -- to falsely blame Republicans for the purpose of taking back the House of

Representatives in the 2014 midterm elections, and continuing his scurrilous efforts to the growth and power of government, unabated.

Our country will surely feel the social, political and economic pain of Obamacareless, hopefully in time for voters to reject the socialist takeover in the 2014 and 2016 elections. Meanwhile, Utah, Arizona and other states are opening the national parks in their states. Indeed, all national parks and federal lands should be turned over to the states to deal with as they wish. A first step in reducing the grip of federal power.

Eliminating the Department of Education should be next, followed by the over-regulating EPA, and adopting the "Fair (consumption) Tax" to abolish the distribution of wealth taxation and the punitive-taxing power of the IRS. Limited government -- as outlined in the Constitution -- should be practiced by our elected representatives, and the electorate should hold them to it.

Riverside Press Enterprise
November 21, 2013

Talking with Iran foolish

It comes as no surprise that President Barack Obama and Secretary of State John Kerry failed in their negotiations with Iran. It should be understood that Iran is using negotiations, delays and distractions to buy time so it can develop nuclear weapons.

Our administration should know that you don't negotiate with terrorists or a terrorist state.

Furthermore, throwing Israel under the bus in order to talk with Iran is unconscionable. Israel is our only friend and ally in the Middle East and a great help in dealing with Iran. Israel has an absolute right to exist.

(Original letter)

Obama administration incompetency, domestic and foreign

With less than 50,000 people signing up for Obamacare on government web sites, and 49,000 on state exchange sites, and half of both have been unable to complete the process, it clearly demonstrates that government is incompetent. Worse, 7 million people have had their health plans cancelled because they don't meet Obamacare standards -- which will more than double or triple their premiums and deductibles -- leads the American people to the inescapable conclusion that President Obama lied, and that the Obamacare law should be renamed, "The Unaffordable Careless Act" -- a tyranny which will ultimately and unnecessarily cost taxpayers an extra $1.2 trillion.

Plus, it comes as no surprise that President Obama and Secretary of State Kerry are foreign policy incompetents in their negotiations with Iran. It is well known and understood that Iran is using negotiations, delay and distractions to buy time for developing nuclear weapons, and that you don't negotiate with terrorists or a terrorist state. Adding insult to injury, throwing Israel under the bus is unconscionable. Israel is our only friend and ally in the Middle East, a deterrent to Iran and they have an absolute right to exist.

San Bernardino Sun
November 8, 2013

California leading way on government decay

It's bad enough that Governor Brown and the Democrat Legislature are selling-out California with $500 billion in long term debt for government pensions and healthcare benefits -- including the $68 billion high speed rail debacle -- and $50 billion in new taxes.

But when the state smothers business, property owners, jobs and the economy with tyrannical regulations -- and embraces economy-crushing Obamacare with all-encompassing "Covered California" health insurance exchanges -- piling on to the Obama administration's punishing edicts, executive orders and EPA regulations, it's simply authoritarian government flying in the face of the state and federal Constitutions.

Coupled with legislative attempts to weaken or eliminate the people's state constitutional rights to voter initiatives, referendums and recall -- and the state's open invitation to budget-busting illegal immigrants and criminals, California is leading the way to corrosive insecurity, economic chaos and bankruptcy.

USA TODAY
October 29, 2013
(Only letter to the editor)

Financial institutions act as a scapegoat

Punishing JP Morgan Chase with billions of dollars in fines and possibly pursuing criminal charges is government tyranny for an economic collapse caused by a government bent on pushing ideology and unaffordable housing at any cost ("$13 billion penalty leaves behind a whale of a problem," Our view. Too big to fail debate, Wednesday).

JP Morgan Chase, other banks, mortgage bankers and lenders, and Fannie Mae and Freddie Mac sold risky mortgage securities as the result of President Carter's Community Reinvestment Act, and the Clinton administration encouraging them to provide affordable housing mortgages to unqualified buyers. That is what caused the housing and finance bubble to burst, resulting in the economic meltdown. Government's reckless interference with free markets and free enterprise was done before the meltdown, and the situation was exacerbated by government after the collapse.

If anyone should be prosecuted, it should be former President Bill Clinton, not JP Morgan.

Daniel B. Jeffs
Apple Valley, Calif.

Daily Press Apple Valley Review
Commentary by Daniel B. Jeffs
October 29, 2013

Obamacare and the socialist agenda

The socialist agenda shifted into high gear with Obamacare. President Obama and the congressional left are making it painfully clear that they intend to complete the socialist agenda with housing, jobs, income redistribution, food and clothing.

Clinton's socialist affordable housing agenda was carried out with forced approval of mortgages for unqualified buyers, which exploded, and collapsed housing and finance in 2008. The same thing is likely to happen with Obamacare, with a direct, negative impact on the people.

Moreover, the Justice Department is using the socialist Dodd-Frank finance law to shake down JP Morgan Chase bank with a $13 billion hit for selling risky mortgage-back securities, when it was government that caused the circumstances, and is now seeking control of banking, CEO salaries and compensation.

President Obama is keeping up the pressure of distractions from Obamacare problems by gearing up a push for immigration reform and amnesty that will weigh even more heavily on taxpayers and the fragile economy. Indeed, it's all targeted by the unyielding socialist agenda.

Prosecute Clinton, not JP Morgan

Punishing JP Morgan with a $13 billion fine and pursuing criminal charges is unconscionable government tyranny for an economic collapse caused by government bent on pushing an ideology and affordable housing at any cost.

JP Morgan Chase, other banks, mortgage bankers and lenders, Fannie Mae and Freddie Mac sold risky mortgage securities as the result of President Carter's Community Reinvestment Act and the Clinton administration forcing them to provide unaffordable housing mortgages to unqualified buyers.

That is what caused the housing and finance bubble to burst, resulting in the 2008 economic meltdown. Government's reckless interference with free markets and free enterprise was done before the meltdown and exacerbated by government after the collapse.

And that is what raised the national debt from $10 trillion to $17 trillion in 5 years, which will reach $20 trillion by 2016 at the hands of President Obama and congressional Democrats, who have prolonged the recession.

If anyone should be prosecuted, it should be former President Bill Clinton for causing the collapse -- and former Rep. Barney Frank and former Sen. Chris Dodd for perpetuating the conditions leading to the meltdown -- not JP Morgan Chase.

Unfortunately, before leaving Congress, Dodd and Frank added insult to injury with the over-reaching Dodd-Frank finance laws.

Daniel B. Jeffs is an Apple Valley resident and author of the series, "Letters to the Editor: From the Trenches of Democracy"

Daily Press
October 25, 2013

Obamacare and socialism

The socialist agenda shifted into high gear with Obamacare. President Obama and the congressional left are making it painfully clear that they intend to complete the socialist agenda with housing, jobs, income redistribution, food and clothing.

Clinton's socialist affordable housing agenda was carried out with forced approval of mortgages for unqualified buyers, which exploded, and collapsed housing and finance in 2008. The same thing is likely to happen with Obamacare, with a direct, negative impact on the people.

Moreover, the Justice Department is using the socialist Dodd-Frank finance law to shake down JP Morgan Chase bank with a $13 billion hit for selling risky mortgage-back securities, when it was government that caused the circumstances, and is now seeking control of banking, CEO salaries and compensation.

President Obama is keeping up the pressure of distractions from Obamacare problems by gearing up a push for immigration reform and amnesty that will weigh even more heavily on taxpayers and the fragile economy. Indeed, it's all targeted by the unyielding socialist agenda.

Daily Press Apple Valley Review
October 22, 2013
Commentary

Obama's extortion worked by Daniel B. Jeffs

Republicans will take more heat than Democrats over President Obama's shutdown extortion and demonizing the tea party. The forced compromise will carry the budget and debt ceiling into next year, leaving Obamacare in place.

But when Obamacare takes hold, Obama and the Democrats will suffer from the costly mess, hopefully enough for Republicans to keep the House and gain back the Senate and the presidency in 2014/16.

Letting Obamacareless and the debt ceiling ride, would raise the national debt to over $20 trillion and take America over the social, political and economic cliff. Mission accomplished by President Obama. Voters can't afford to let that happen.

Daniel B. Jeffs is an Apple Valley resident and author of the series, "Letters to the Editor: From the Trenches of Democracy

San Diego Union-Tribune
October 19, 2013

When Obamacare takes hold, we all suffer

Republicans will take more heat than Democrats over President Obama's shutdown extortion and demonizing the tea party. The forced compromise will carry the budget and debt ceiling into next year, leaving Obamacare in place.

But when Obamacare takes hold, Obama and the Democrats will suffer from the costly mess, hopefully enough for Republicans to keep the House and gain back the Senate and the presidency in 2014 an 2016.

Letting Obamacareless and the debt ceiling ride, would raise the national debt to over $20 trillion and take America over the social, political and economic cliff. Mission accomplished by President Obama.

Voter's can't afford to let that happen.

Daily Press Apple Valley Review
October 15, 2013
Commentary

California in double-trouble by Daniel B. Jeffs

Californians are in the grip of government double-trouble, with Governor Brown and a Democrat Legislature -- plus President Obama and former House Democrat Speaker/Minority leader, Nancy Pelosi -- using the liberal-media propaganda machine to drive the socialist justice agenda from the golden-state coast to the Eastern seaboard.

It's bad enough that Governor Brown and the Democrat Legislature are selling-out California with $500 billion in long term debt for government pensions and healthcare benefits -- including the $100 billion high speed rail debacle -- and $50 billion in new taxes.

But when the state smothers business, property owners, jobs and the economy with tyrannical regulations -- and embraces economy-crushing Obamacare with all-encompassing "Covered California" health insurance exchanges -- piling on to the Obama administration's punishing edicts, executive orders and EPA regulations, it's simply authoritarian government flying in the face of the state and federal Constitutions.

Coupled with legislative attempts to weaken or eliminate the people's state constitutional rights to voter initiatives, referendums and recall -- and the state's open invitation to budget-busting illegal immigrants and criminals, California is leading the way to corrosive insecurity, economic chaos and bankruptcy.

Will of the people ignored

When President Obama ran for the Oval Office he promised to fundamentally transform America and resolve a health care crisis that -- other than Medicare and Medicaid fraud, waste and abuse -- did not exist. Unfortunately for the American people, he is keeping those unconscionable promises.

After his election, President Obama and the Democrat Congress rammed through economy-busting Obamacare without debate. This tyrannical act was rejected by the majority of voters who gave control of the their House of Representatives to Republicans in the 2010 mid-term elections. The Supreme Court betrayed the people by ruling that Obamacare was constitutional because it was a tax, rather than what it really is: fees and penalties for failure to comply.

House attempts to repeal or modify Obamacare have been met by President Obama's complicit media blitz against Republicans -- demonizing patriotic tea party Republicans -- issuing edicts and executive orders -- and shutting down select government services to blackmail Republicans with false accusations. Coupled with the tyranny of Senate Majority Leader Harry Reid, the President and the Democrat-controlled Senate are blatantly ignoring the Constitution and the will of the people.

If we are to protect ourselves from becoming a giant underclass and social, political and economic doom, voters must elect a Republican government in 2014 and 2016.

Daniel B. Jeffs is an Apple Valley resident and author of the series, "Letters to the Editor: From the Trenches of Democracy

San Diego Union-Tribune
October 11, 2013

California in double-trouble

Californians are in the grip of government double-trouble, with Governor Brown and a Democrat Legislature -- plus President Obama and former House Democrat Speaker/Minority leader,

Nancy Pelosi -- using the liberal-media propaganda machine to drive the socialist justice agenda from the golden-state coast to the Eastern Seaboard.

It's bad enough that Governor Brown and the Democrat Legislature are selling-out California with $500 billion in long term debt for government pensions and healthcare benefits, including the $100 billion high speed rail debacle and $50 billion in new taxes.

But when the state smothers business, property owners, jobs and the economy with tyrannical regulations -- and embraces economy-crushing Obamacare with all-encompassing "Covered California" health insurance exchanges -- piling on to the Obama administration's punishing edicts, executive orders and EPA regulations, it's simply authoritarian government flying in the face of the state and federal Constitutions.

Coupled with legislative attempts to weaken or eliminate the people's state constitutional rights to voter initiatives, referendums and recall -- and the state's open invitation to budget-busting illegal immigrants and criminals, California is leading the way to corrosive insecurity, economic chaos and bankruptcy.

Riverside Press Enterprise
October 11, 2013

Obama ignores people

When President Obama ran for the Oval Office he promised to fundamentally transform America and resolve a health care crisis that did not exist. Unfortunately for the American people, he is keeping those unconscionable promises.

After his election, he and the Democrats in Congress rammed through economy-busting Obamacare.

This tyrannical act was rejected by the majority of voters who gave control of the their House of Representatives to Republicans in the 2010 midterm elections.

Obama reacted to House attempts to repeal or modify Obamacare by demonizing patriotic tea party Republicans, issuing edicts and executive orders and shutting down select government services to blackmail Republicans.

Coupled with the tyranny of Senate Majority Leader Harry Reid, the President and the Democrat-controlled Senate are blatantly ignoring the Constitution and the will of the people.

If we are to protect ourselves from becoming a giant underclass of people, we must elect a Republican government in 2014 and 2016.

(original letter)

Will of the people ignored

When President Obama ran for the Oval Office he promised to fundamentally transform America and resolve a health care crisis that did not exist. Unfortunately for the American people, he is keeping those unconscionable promises.

After his election, President Obama and the Democrat Congress rammed through economy-busting Obamacare without debate. This tyrannical act was rejected by the majority of voters who gave control of the their House of Representatives to Republicans in the 2010 mid-term elections. The Supreme Court betrayed the people by ruling that Obamacare was constitutional because it was a tax, rather than what it really is: fees and penalties for failure to comply.

House attempts to repeal or modify Obamacare have been met by President Obama's complicit media blitz against Republicans -- demonizing patriotic tea party Republicans -- issuing edicts and executive orders -- and shutting down select government services to blackmail Republicans with false accusations. Coupled with the tyranny of Senate Majority Leader Harry Reid, the President and the Democrat-controlled Senate are blatantly ignoring the Constitution and the will of the people.

If we are to protect ourselves from becoming a giant underclass and social, political and economic doom, voters must elect a Republican government in 2014 and 2016.

Daily Press Apple Valley Review
October 8, 2013

The deleterious Obama-effect by Daniel B. Jeffs

President Obama's perpetual campaign against the best interests of America is manifested by his obsession with his so-called "signature legislation" of the UnAffordable Health Care Act -- his "Social Justice" assault on the fragile economy -- his leading from behind bungling of foreign policy highlighted by deals with the devils of Russia and Iran, and ignoring the growing monsters of terrorism.

Too many 2008 and 2012 presidential election voters were oblivious to the deleterious effect of President Obama's promise to fundamentally transform America -- the Clinton-caused housing and financial meltdown -- and the puppet-Democrat Congress and the biased media, which propelled him to do just that with Obamacare, edicts and executive orders, runaway spending and unsustainable debt. That is what created the Tea Party, polarized America, extended the recession and fortunately, raised the influence of Fox News.

Obamacare, reckless spending and debt limit madness are being perpetuated by Democrats demonizing the Tea Party, and Republicans eating their own. That's why I am an independent voter. Truth is, the spontaneous Tea Party represents the feelings of the majority of Americans. Hopefully, sanity, social and economic recovery, and national security will be restored after the 2014 and 2016 elections. Anything less could result in the final fall of the greatest nation on earth.

Daniel B. Jeffs is an Apple Valley resident and author of the series, "Letters to the Editor: From the Trenches of Democracy

NEWSMAX MAGAZINE
October 2013 issue

No-plan president

President Obama's budget plan, along with his targeted sequester, can only be described as unconscionable deceptions, intimidation and petty political extortion at the expense of the economy and the middle class ("GOP Day of Reckoning as Sequester Showdown Looms," September).

He has no budget plan at all. Budgets require a positive outcome and expenditures. Instead, the president is acting like an irresponsible child with a no-limit taxpayer credit card.

Daily Press Apple Valley Review
October 1, 2013

President Obama: Presidential pretender and constitutional offender by Daniel B. Jeffs

Lest voters forget, presidential candidate, Senator Obama campaigned to fundamentally transform America, declaring a healthcare crisis when there was none, and promising that electricity rates would necessarily skyrocket to accomplish his green energy conversion -- regardless of the housing and financial collapse, economic meltdown and massive job losses.

After President Obama's election, his process to fundamentally transform America began by ramming his Affordable Healthcare Act (AKA Obamacare -- unaffordable careless act) through the Democrat-controlled Congress without objection from his political lemmings, passed wasteful stimulus spending, raised the national debt to unsustainable levels, and continues to diminish America's standing in the world.

After Democrats lost the House of Representative to the Republicans, Mr. Obama set about to unconstitutionally circumvent Congress with edicts and executive orders to pursue green energy at the expense of the oil industry and the coal energy industry, with EPA carbon enforcement and shutting down oil exploration and production on federal lands and offshore.

Of course the other shoe is about to drop on the economy with the implementation of Obamacare -- the circumvention of Congress and the Constitution continuing unabated -- as President Obama goes about the business of perpetual lies and deceit, political pontificating and campaigning to transform America at the expense of our freedoms, our economy, our foreign policy, our allies, our national security and our future.

Surely, Mr. Obama's legacy will be that of being a presidential pretender, manipulator-in-chief, and serial constitutional offender.

Daniel B. Jeffs is an Apple Valley resident and author of the series, "Letters to the Editor: From the Trenches of Democracy."

San Bernardino Sun
October 1, 2013

Obama's deal with the Russian devil

President Obama and Vladimir Putin cooked up the deal for Syria to turn over chemical weapons to make them both look good. Recall Obama told Putin that he would be more flexible after his re-election. If Obama is flexible with Putin on the chemical weapons, Russia and Iran win, America loses, as does our national security.

Syria is not the deciding issue here. Putin's Russia is. They provided chemical weapons to Syria, Egypt and the Middle East.

Putin and Iran are the main threat to our economy, our national security and the world. Iran undermined all of our efforts in Iraq and Afghanistan, making our losses futile.

Backed By Russia, Iran's design is to control the Middle East and North Africa, and to command the forces of radical Islam with nuclear power. We must stand with Israel and all our combined powers to prevent that from happening. Difficult, when our President sells-out to Putin and makes deals with the devil.

Lest we forget, Vladimir Putin is on course to recover Russia's power in the World, and along with China, replace America as the planet's only super economic and military power.

San Diego Union-Tribune
September 30, 2013

The deleterious Obama-effect

President Obama's perpetual campaign against the best interests of America is manifested by his obsession with his so-called "signature legislation" of the UnAffordable Health Care Act -- his "Social Justice" assault on the fragile economy -- his leading from behind bungling of foreign policy highlighted by deals with the devils of Russia and Iran, and ignoring the growing monsters of terrorism.

Too many 2008 and 2012 presidential election voters were oblivious to the deleterious effect of President Obama's promise to fundamentally transform America -- the Clinton-caused housing and financial meltdown -- and the puppet-Democrat Congress and the biased media, which propelled him to do just that with Obamacare, edicts and executive orders, runaway spending and unsustainable debt. That is what created the Tea Party, polarized America, extended the recession and fortunately, raised the influence of Fox News.

Obamacare, reckless spending and debt limit madness are being perpetuated by Democrats demonizing the Tea Party, and Republicans eating their own. That's why I am an independent voter. Truth is, the spontaneous Tea Party represents the feelings of the majority of Americans. Hopefully, sanity, social and economic recovery, and national security will be restored after the 2014 and 2016 elections. Anything less could result in the final fall of the greatest nation on earth.

Daily Press Apple Valley Review
September 24, 2013

Deals with the devil by Daniel B. Jeffs

President Obama and Vladimir Putin cooked up the deal for Syria to turn over chemical weapons to make them both look good. Recall Obama told Putin that he would be more flexible after his re-election.

If Obama is flexible with Putin on the chemical weapons, Russia and Iran win, America loses, as does our national security.

Syria is not the deciding issue here. Putin's Russia is. They provided chemical weapons to Syria, Egypt and the Middle East. Putin and Iran are the main threat to our economy, our national security and the world. Iran undermined all of our efforts in Iraq and Afghanistan, making our losses futile.

Backed by Russia, Iran's design is to control the Middle East and North Africa, and to command the forces of radical Islam with nuclear power. We must stand with Israel and all our combined powers to prevent that from happening. Difficult, when our President sells out to Putin and makes deals with the devil.

Lest we forget, Vladimir Putin is on course to recover Russia's power in the World, and along with China, replace America as the planet's only super economic and military power.

Daniel B. Jeffs is an Apple Valley Resident and the author of the book series, Letters to the Editor: From the Trenches of Democracy

San Diego Union-Tribune
September 23, 2013

Presidential pretender, constitutional offender

Lest voters forget, presidential candidate, Senator Obama campaigned to fundamentally transform America, declaring a healthcare crisis when there was none, and promising that electricity rates would necessarily skyrocket to accomplish his green energy conversion -- regardless of the housing and financial collapse, economic meltdown and massive job losses.

After President Obama's election, his process to fundamentally transform America began by ramming his Affordable Healthcare Act (AKA Obamacare -- unaffordable careless act) through the Democrat-controlled Congress without objection from his political lemmings, passed wasteful stimulus spending, raised the national debt to unsustainable levels, and continues to diminish America's standing in the world.

After Democrats lost the House of Representative to the Republicans, Mr. Obama set about to unconstitutionally circumvent Congress with edicts and executive orders to pursue green energy at the expense of the oil industry and the coal energy industry, with EPA carbon enforcement and shutting down oil exploration and production on federal lands and offshore.

Of course the other shoe is about to drop on the economy with the implementation of Obamacare -- the circumvention of Congress and the Constitution continuing unabated -- as President Obama goes about the business of perpetual lies and deceit, political pontificating and campaigning to transform America at the expense of our freedoms, our economy, our foreign policy, our allies, our national security and our future.

Surely, Mr. Obama's legacy will be that of being a presidential pretender, manipulator-in-chief, and serial constitutional offender.

Riverside Press Enterprise
September 20, 2013

Bow to Russia? No

I think President Barack Obama and Russian President Vladimir Putin cooked up the deal for Syria to turn over its chemical weapons to make them both look good.

Remember when Obama, unaware his words were being recorded, was caught telling outgoing Russian President Dmitry Medvedev that he would have "more flexibility" regarding things like missile defense after the 2012 elections?

If Obama is flexible with Putin on the chemical weapons, Russia and Iran win, and America loses.

Syria is not the issue here. Putin is. Russia is providing weapons to a number of nations in the Middle East, including Syria. Russia is also forming an alliance with Iran.

Iran and Russia are the main threat to our and the world's security. Backed By Russia, Iran aims to control the Middle East and

North Africa and command the forces of radical Islam with nuclear power.

We must stand with Israel and prevent this from happening. But that will be difficult when our President sells out to Putin and makes deals with the devil.

San Diego Union-Tribune
September 19, 2013

Military security failures

The DC Navy Yard massacre of 12 employees and Navy personnel by crazed former Navy reservist, Aaron Alexis sends another frightful message to America:

Lack of leadership and attention to military screening and security allowed Army Maj. Nidal Malik Hasan to carry out the massacre of soldiers at Fort Hood, and Aaron Alexis to enter the Navy Yard with a weapon to begin his murderous rampage.

The same security failures apply to the treasonous release of military secrets by Army Pvt. Bradley Manning, and NSA secrets by contractor Edward Snowden -- all of which substantially increases threats to our national security.

San Bernardino Sun
September 5, 2013

Obama's leaderless foreign policy

President Obama's leaderless foreign policy presidency has given al-Qaida and the Muslim Brotherhood their rise to power in the Middle East and North Africa, leaving Muslim nations in mass confusion and costing thousands of lives. Obama's missile-man approach in dealing with our mortal enemy has escalated their invasions and emboldened their threat to our national security.

Egypt and Libya are bloody examples of the Obama administration's incompetence. Israel must be feeling a substantial increase in the threat against them, particularly from Iran, Syria and their Hezbollah army of terrorists.

Bombing Syria over the use of chemical weapons on its own people would only serve to escalate the violence and more aggression from Iran, which would likely spill over into assaults on Israel. Clearly, President Obama's focus must be in support of Israel, against Iran's nuclear weapons threat, and the overall threat to our national security, by any means necessary. Unfortunately, Obama's obsession with the growth of government and weakening America is more frightening.

(Original letter)

President Obama's leaderless foreign policy presidency has given al-Qaeda and the Muslim Brotherhood their rise to power in the Middle East and North Africa, leaving Muslim nations in mass confusion and costing thousands of lives. Surely, Obama's missile-man approach in dealing with our mortal enemy has done little to nothing against terrorists. Rather, it has escalated their invasions and emboldened their threat to our national security.

Egypt and Libya are bloody examples of the Obama administration's incompetence. Allowing the assassination of our Ambassador and other Americans in Benghazi, Libya -- and Egypt to fall by supporting the Muslim Brotherhood and President Morsi was a deadly mistake -- saved only by the strength of Egypt's military. Certainly, Israel must be feeling a substantial increase in the threat against them, particularly from Iran, Syria and their Hezbollah army of terrorists.

Bombing Syria over the use of chemical weapons on its own people would only serve to escalate the violence and more aggression from Iran, which would likely spill over into assaults on Israel. Clearly, President Obama's focus must be in support of Israel, against Iran's nuclear weapons threat, and the overall threat to our national security, by any means necessary. Unfortunately, Obama's obsession with the growth of government and weakening America is more frightening.

The Wall Street Journal
September 4, 2013
(Lead Letter of 5 letters)

Remembering and Fulfilling Dr. King's Great Dream

Regarding your editorial "Government and Segregation" (Aug. 29): Commemorations of the 1963 march on Washington have fallen short. President Obama could be the driving force in realizing Martin Luther King Jr.'s dream by turning around problems in African-American communities by condemning the violent gang, rap and drug culture, calling for family values and stability, personal responsibility, self-reliance, skill training and serious education reform.

President Obama missed that opportunity. He could have stressed these issues to his fellow African-Americans and their misguided leaders and then follow through with it for the remainder of his term. As the first black president, that could be President Obama's major legacy, finalizing what Martin Luther King accomplished.

San Diego Union-Tribune
September 3, 2013

Big jump in fast food pay is a bad idea

My first job out of high school was at the first McDonald's in Downey in 1957, and I was happy to get it. My high school sweetheart and future wife's first job was at Foster Freeze. One of our son's first jobs was at a Carl's Jr. and our daughter worked at a Subway Sandwich in Apple Valley. Learning those first job skills, responsibilities and self reliance were vital to our future success.

We need reign in the SEIU union, which is now organizing fast-food workers with the unconscionable notion of doubling their entry-level minimum wage. It will hurt the small business franchises of McDonald's, Burger King, Wendy's, Taco Bell and all the others, and in the end will harm the workers, raise the cost of food, reduce jobs, and hurt low income consumers who depend on low-cost meals.

Daily Press Apple Valley Review
September 3, 2013
Op-Ed by Daniel B. Jeffs

SEIU puts entry-level jobs at risk

Surely, we need reign in the self-corruption of big government tied to big unions, such as the SEIU -- now organizing young, innocent fast food workers with the untenable notion of doubling their entry-level minimum wage -- which will hurt the small business franchises of McDonald's, Burger King, Wendy's, Taco Bell and all the others -- and in the end will hurt the workers, raise the cost of food, reduce jobs, and hurt low income consumers who depend on low cost meals. The fast food industry has long-provided valuable entry-level work for millions, which is being put at risk in an already failing economy.

My first job out of high school was at the first McDonald's in Downey, California in 1957, and I was happy to get it. My high school sweetheart and future wife's first job was at Foster Freeze. One of our son's first jobs was at a new Carl's Jr. and our daughter worked at a Subway Sandwich shop in Apple Valley, California in the 1980's. Learning those first job skills, a work ethic, responsibilities and self reliance were vital to our future success. Our son built a successful business and our daughter is on the executive staff in the federal prison system.

After working at McDonald's, I worked at a tire shop, a fiberglass laminating shop, on the assembly line at a GM plant, in aerospace as a laminator and draftsman -- and subsequently went on to a 41-year career in law enforcement and the criminal justice system. I watched the liberal/progressive ideology rip the heart out of public education, the workplace, government, traditional morals, the family, society, our founding principles, the rule of law, and our nation as a whole.

Indeed, when liberal social justice tyrants takeover education, government, unions, business and industry with over-regulation, punishing taxes on small business and personal success, while runaway government spending and insurmountable debt go on unabated

-- driving our country on a fast track to ruin -- it's time to put on the breaks and just say, "No more."

Daniel B. Jeffs is a resident of Apple Valley and the author of: *Letters to the Editor: From the Trenches of Democracy*

New York Post
September 2, 2013

King's dream could be realized by Obama

Commemorations of the 1963 march on Washington fell short. Indeed, Obama could be the driving force in realizing King's dream if he worked to solve problems in African-American communities,

He could have done so by condemning the violent gang and drug cultures, calling for family values and stability, personal responsibility, self-reliance, skills training and serious education reform.

Obama missed that opportunity in his address to the nation at the Lincoln Memorial. He could have stressed these issues to the African-American community and its leaders, and followed through with it for the remainder of his term.

As the first black president, that could have been Obama's major legacy: finalizing what King accomplished.

Daily Press Dispatch
August 25, 2013

Bill Clinton caused the housing, financial meltdown

Phil Gramm and Mike Solon's somewhat restrained analysis of the cause of the housing and financial crisis in the Wall Street Journal is at least a published account of the direct, real cause of the housing and financial crash, which was former president Bill Clinton's administration.

Indeed, Clinton abused his power by using President Carter's ill-conceived Community Reinvestment Act to force affordable housing into the housing market by any means necessary.

Clinton's wrecking crew, HUD Secretary Andrew Cuomo and Attorney General Janet Reno abused their power by forcing Fannie Mae and Freddie Mac to give home loans to unqualified buyers, and threatened Banks and mortgage lenders to do the same -- which led to subprime loans, bundling, credit-default swaps, and sales of contaminated government-backed home loan securities -- which infected Wall Street and the world economy.

Of course, House and Senate Finance Committee heavyweights, Rep. Barney Frank and Sen. Christopher Dodd perpetuated the looming housing and financial crash with lies and deceit about the safety and soundness of the affordable housing loans, to continue the liberal Democrat agenda of social justice at any cost.

Alas, that cost is costing America's economy and all of us housing losses and jobs, aggravated by punishing taxes and regulations, runaway spending and unsustainable debt -- frustrated by President Obama's tyrannical government growth and the growing threat to our national security.

USA TODAY
August 22, 2013

Put renewable fuel quotas in rearview mirror

USA TODAY got it right in the analysis of the senseless, obsolete need for the increased ethanol mandate ("Rising ethanol quotas pump more money from your pocket," Our view, energy independence debate, Friday).

Indeed, corn ethanol has become another poster idea for the costly failures of government's good intentions. It's bad enough that ethanol is unnecessary for our vehicles that are becoming more fuel efficient and that increased domestic oil and gas production makes ethanol mandates even more costly and unnecessary.

It is unconscionable for Congress not to admit the mistake and repeal all corn ethanol additive mandates.

Alas, that's why government growth, spending and debt are consuming our freedoms and our future. If we are to survive, voters must reign in and reverse the insanity in the 2014 and 2016 elections.

VV Daily Press
August 22, 2013

Dump corn ethanol

USA TODAY and WSJ editorials are correct about the senseless increased ethanol mandate and the obsolete need for ethanol in America. Indeed, corn ethanol fuel has become another poster idea for the costly failures of government's good intentions and the bad intentions of the big corn ethanol industry.

Surely, it's bad enough that corn ethanol is not only unnecessary for our vehicles that are becoming more fuel efficient, that increased domestic oil and gas production makes ethanol mandates even more costly and unnecessary, and that corn ethanol is robbing our corn supply -- raising the cost of food.

It is simply unconscionable for Congress not to admit the mistake and repeal all corn ethanol additive mandates. Particularly, when ethanol ruins the engines in our vehicles, it is more toxic than gasoline emissions, and even California asked for an exemption to using ethanol.

But that's politics and big government, isn't it? Pass bad laws, invoke punishing taxes and regulations, and let it ride. Alas, that's why government growth, spending and debt are consuming our freedoms and our future. If we are to survive, voters must reign in and reverse the insanity.

Riverside Press Enterprise
August 14, 2013

President breaking U.S.

President Barack Obama making exceptions for unions and congressional staff regarding Obamacare, along with delaying implementation of it until after the 2014 elections, comes as no surprise.

Obama continues to circumvent our nation's laws executive orders and edicts. And these orders end up hurting the middle class.

And lest we forget, this debacle was created by him when he ran in the 2008 election, telling everyone there was a crisis in health care. He created a crisis that didn't exist. Of course the crisis that did exist, and persists, is the Democrat-caused housing and financial crash.

Health care in America needed some work, but not with national health care that will surely break our economic back. The Democrat-controlled Congress that rammed it through also shares the blame.

(original letter)

Breaking America's economic back

Illegally exempting unions and congressional staff from Obamacare, along with pushing the implementation until after the 2014 elections comes as no surprise.

Particularly when President Obama continues to circumvent the law with EPA and Energy executive orders and edicts destined to hurt the middle class.

Lest we forget, the president's Obamacareless monster was created by then Senator Obama while running in the 2008 election. He created a crisis that didn't exist. Of course the crisis that did exist, and persists, is the Clinton/Frank/Dodd Democrat-caused housing and financial crash.

Healthcare in America needed some work, but not with national health care that will surely break our economic back. The Democrat Congress that rammed it through without debate, shares the blame. Indeed, every House and Senate member who voted for it.

Daily Press/Apple Valley Review
August 13, 2013

Snowden, Manning, Hasan are traitors

There is no question that Edward Snowden is a traitor for revealing NSA secrets aiding our mortal enemy Islamic terrorists. Indeed,

Army Pvt. Manning is a traitor for doing the same with classified material concerning Iraq and Afghanistan, and Army Major Nidal Hasan is murderous a traitor for assassinating our troops at Fort Hood being processed for a tour of duty in Afghanistan.

The problem is, none of these blatant traitors are being prosecuted for treason, which Is the historical product of our cowardly liberal government's unwritten policy of "none dare call it treason." Of course the Snowden, Manning and Hasan cases were exacerbated by President Obama's weakness with China and Russia, and the screening and security failures of the CIA, NSA and the U.S. Army allowing the traitors to operate in their respective positions.

Nonetheless, all three should be convicted of treason, punishable by either death or life in prison and the loss of citizenship. Surely, their open contempt for the privilege of being a United States citizen is an indictment of how casual and cynical too many people have become about being American and the freedom that goes along with it, including President Obama.

Alas, Obama's blind obsession with forcing social justice in America and his narcissistic ill-perceived leadership in the world -- at the expense of our economy, our freedoms and our national security -- abandoning Israel, Iran's nuclear threat, and the al-Qaeda/Muslim Brotherhood takeover of the Middle East and North Africa -- and their Jihadist agenda for terrorist attacks against America and the West -- makes him the greatest threat to our future and our survival.

San Bernardino Sun
August 8, 2013

Obama's speeches distract from his failures

President Obama's perpetual campaign continues with the latest round of biased media-supported, staged travel-trivia speeches -- stroking the economy and the middle class -- with his clueless people backdrops of bobbleheads nodding and applauding his every point, on cue.

Of course, Obama's latest charges against his Republican opponents -- of causing Washington to take its eye off the ball with "distractions, political posturing and phony scandals" -- are in fact his phony-in-chief maneuvers to detract from his abusive government, social, political, economic and national security failures.

Meanwhile, the president relentlessly continues his unprecedented abuse of power, executive orders and edicts, political appointments, and administrative regulations forcing his destructive injustice, miseducation, energy, environmental, healthcare, immigration, financial, debt and spending agenda upon America.

NewsMax Magazine
August 2013 Issue

Self-radicalized Terrorists

There is no question that the Obama administration endangers our national security. President Obama and Attorney General Eric Holder are making it painfully clear that they had no problem risking our national security by cutting off the FBI questioning of Boston bomber, Dzhokhar Tsarnaev.

They, along with a federal magistrate that stopped the questioning of Tsarnaev, are abdicating their sworn duty to defend our public safety against all enemies, foreign and domestic, leaving them with the blood of Boston on their hands. That, along with failures against Islamic Fort Hood and Benghazi terrorism amount to unconscionable aid and comfort to our enemies and is tantamount to impeachable treason.

San Diego Union-Tribune
July 22, 2013

President inflames Zimmerman anger

President Obama's Trayvon Martin-driven remarks regarding race do little to nothing to relieve tensions brought on by the intense radical African-American leaders' reaction to George Zimmerman's not guilty verdict that resulted in a national call to protest the perceived injustice of justice being served in the Florida court. Indeed, the president failed to recognize or condemn the violence, and did nothing to dispel the self-inflicted stereotype.

Alas, lest we forget, the Trayvon Martin/George Zimmerman conflict was not black and white. It was black and Hispanic.

(original letter)
The most divisive president
President Obama's Trayvon Martin-driven remarks regarding race do little to nothing to relieve tensions brought on by the intense radical African-American leaders' reaction to George Zimmerman's "Not Guilty" verdict that resulted in a national call to protest the perceived injustice of justice being served in the Florida court. Indeed, the president failed to recognize or condemn the violence, and did nothing to dispel the self-inflicted stereotype.

In fact, President Obama's divisive racial statements exacerbated the resulting violence and rioting in the streets of Los Angeles and elsewhere with gangs of African-American juveniles and young adults assaulting and robbing innocent people, looting stores and setting fires -- including two American flags. Indeed, now there is another media-driven Al Sharpton-Jesse Jackson move to protest in 100 major cities across America.

Alas, lest we forget, the Trayvon Martin/George Zimmerman conflict was not black and white. It was black and Hispanic.

Clearly, America has been placed in deepening social, political and economic stress, chaos and deterioration by the most divisive president in our history. One who's blind social justice political agenda -- supported by congressional Democrats -- has grown government with a tyrannical war against free market Capitalism, imposing economy-crushing national health care, costly green energy, spending, insurmountable debt, abused his personal power and abdicated our national security.

Daily Press
July 19, 2013
Re: Marching for Trayvon

Verdict should end it

There is absolutely no excuse for African-American teenagers protesting the tragic death of Trayvon Martin and the acquittal of George Zimmerman to shut down the Mall, jump on cars, assault people and steal from a convenience store. Coupled with gangs of juveniles rioting, looting, damaging property, and setting fires -- including burning two American flags (one up a flag pole) -- on Crenshaw Boulevard in Los Angeles and mugging people on Hollywood Boulevard were blatant exercises in hate, racism and terrorism.

African American leaders Al Sharpton, Jesse Jackson and others exploited Trayvon's death in the unconscionable exercise of their power to incite demonstrations and rioting all across the nation -- labeling the death as racist, when it was not.

The entire Trayvon/Zimmerman madness was, and still is, media-driven. George Zimmerman's life is in danger and it has been destroyed by insidious persecution. If anyone should be prosecuted further, it should be Sharpton, Jackson and others for inciting to riot and for making the young black male stereotype they vehemently protest, a reality. They have bullied America into believing they are untouchable sacred cows. Our free society doesn't work that way. If they hate America that much, they are free to leave.

Daily Press Apple Valley Review
July 16, 2013

President Obama: Constitutional violator

President Obama violated the Article II, Section 3 Constitutional duty that the president "shall take care that the laws be faithfully executed," with his failure to execute the activation of the health care employer mandate law by delay -- which was obviously done to avoid 2014 mid-term election problems.

Indeed, failing to faithfully execute laws is nothing new for the president, who has habitually failed to execute illegal immigration laws, and to secure our borders, leaving us vulnerable to the increased invasion of criminals and terrorists.

Worse, President Obama has abused his power by creating laws by executive order and edict to the Dept. of Interior, the Energy Dept. and with EPA administrative laws to further his green energy agenda with unreasonable fees and punishing taxes.

Taken together, President Obama's tyrannical "unaffordable health careless act" -- and his relentless assaults on our nation's affordable oil and coal energy resources -- will surely drive our economy ever deeper into debt and decline.

Clearly, when one man -- President Obama -- and one Party -- Democrat -- cause our country and our people to live steeped in social, political, economic and national security fear and uncertainty, the 2014 mid-term and 2016 presidential elections will surely become a reckoning for our future.

San Bernardino Sun
July 16, 2013

'Exploitainment' distracts from real threats to U.S.

Relatively innocent fright movies such as Dracula, Wolfman, The Thing, The Blob, Attack of the Body Snatchers, War of the Worlds, Star Wars, Psycho and The Walking Dead have evolved into the exploitainment proliferation of violent extremes in video games, movie and television series, vampires, werewolves, zombies and apocalypse and techno/mechanical end of the world frauds, such as World War Z and Pacific Rim.

It's bad enough that the abandoned and malignant hearts of Hollywood abdicate quality television, movies and social responsibility with lazy, shallow minds, absent original thought to feed their selfish interests by exploiting the emotions of children, juveniles and immature young adults. But when they violate the innocence of children's stories from Snow White to the Lone Ranger with multiple insults, lies and distortions, it's simply unconscionable.

Worse, romanticizing fictional evil, attacks on nonexistent Presidents and the White House, promoting social and political charlatans as liberal saviors, and relentlessly grinding away at mythical corporate demons is stale and spiteful nonsense. There are no zombies, vampires, werewolves, world=ending aliens, monster machines or corporations. Our world deterioration comes from dictators, Communism, Socialists, and the greater threat from Islamic Jihadists bent on the elimination of infidels and ruling the World.

Riverside Press Enterprise
July 10, 1013

Recall Harris, Brown

Attorney General Kamala Harris continued her activism on behalf of homosexual causes by requesting that the stay on same-sex unions be immediately lifted in California following the Supreme Court's ruling on Prop. 8 ("Gay marriages resume," June 29).

Once it was lifted, she then went ton to preside over a gay wedding. This is outrageous malfeasance.

Gov. Jerry Brown and Harris violated their oaths of office by refusing to defend Prop. 8 simply because their personal agendas were against the will of the people who voted to prohibit gay marriage.

Worse, the Supreme Court betrayed democracy and the Constitution by saying the sponsors of Prop. 8 did not have legal standing to appeal.

And this was after the ballot measure was struck down by Vaughn Walker, a gay federal judge in San Francisco.

How was it not a conflict of interest for Walker to hear the matter?

The decisions against the majority of California voters were unconstitutional and unconscionable.

(original letter)

Recall Attorney General Kamala Harris and Governor Brown

Attorney General Kamala Harris continued her gay activism by asking the federal 9th Circuit to lift its stay immediately, which was done, then performing the first gay marriage in California -- which is outrageous malfeasance.

It didn't matter that former Attorney General, now Governor Jerry Brown and Attorney General Kamala Harris violated their oaths of office by refusing to defend Proposition 8 simply because their personal agendas were against the will of the people, who passed the state constitutional amendment by a 52 percent vote, prohibiting gay marriage -- which was over 7 million voters in a nearly 80 percent voter turnout. Harris and Brown should be recalled.

Worse, Chief Justice Roberts and the Supreme Court majority betrayed democracy and the Constitution by saying the sponsors of Proposition 8 did not have legal standing to appeal after the ballot measure was struck down by Vaughn Walker, a gay federal judge in San Francisco, which was a conflict of interest. Both decisions against the majority of California voters were unconstitutional and unconscionable.

The proponents of Proposition 8 did have standing. In a final appeal to stop the marriages, they were maliciously denied by Justice Kennedy as was the institution of marriage.

San Bernardino Sun
July 4, 2013

Democrat-voter-and-fed-assisted economic suicide

California's AB-32 cap-and-tax revenues - which are supposed to fund green energy programs -- will be diverted by Gov. Brown and the Democrat Legislature to increase Welfare and Medicaid funding by $500 million this year, and the diversions will increase to between $ 2 billion and $15 billion by 2015.

It doesn't seem to matter that the Democrat legislature's recently passed $96.3 billion state budget does nothing to address California's enormous debt. Or that embracing the fraud of Obamacare will raise insurance rates for all Californians, increase the cost of living and decrease employment.

Adding insult to injury, and new federal mandates for increased ethanol in gasoline will raise gas prices, destroy auto and diesel engines, and increase air pollution with insidious toxins. Plus, the increase of corn-ethanol will raise food prices significantly.

Sadly, with Democrat-voter-and-fed-assisted economic suicide in the works, California will surely go into a long political tailspin, nose-dive and crash.

Los Angeles Times
July 2, 2013

Letters: Love and the courts

California Atty. Gen Kamala Harris played the role of an activist by calling on the 9th Circuit to lift its stay immediately, which it did.

It didn't matter to her that she herself and her predecessor, Jerry Brown, now the governor, violated their oaths of office by refusing to defend Proposition 8, which passed in 2008 with the support of more than 7 million voters. Harris and Brown deserve to be recalled.

Worse, the Supreme Court betrayed democracy and the Constitution by saying that the sponsors of Proposition 8 did not have legal standing to appeal. This decision against the majority of voters was unconscionable.

Proposition 8's proponents did have standing. In a final appeal to stop the marriages, they were denied, as was the institution of marriage.

(original letter)

Recall Attorney General Kamala Harris and Governor Brown

Attorney General Kamala Harris continued her gay activism by asking the federal 9th Circuit to lift its stay immediately, which was done, then performing the first gay marriage in California -- which is outrageous malfeasance.

It didn't matter that former Attorney General, now Governor Jerry Brown and Attorney General Kamala Harris violated their oaths of office by refusing to defend Proposition 8 simply because their personal agendas were against the will of the people, who passed the state constitutional amendment by a 52 percent vote, prohibiting gay marriage -- which was over 7 million voters in a nearly 80 percent voter turnout. Harris and Brown should be recalled.

Worse, Chief Justice Roberts and the Supreme Court majority betrayed democracy and the Constitution by saying the sponsors of Proposition 8 did not have legal standing to appeal after the ballot measure was struck down by Vaughn Walker, a gay federal judge in San Francisco, which was a conflict of interest. Both decisions against the majority of California voters were unconstitutional and unconscionable.

The proponents of Proposition 8 did have standing. In a final appeal to stop the marriages, they were maliciously denied by Justice Kennedy as was the institution of marriage.

The New York Post
July 1, 2013

Tearing down tradition: Court's attack on marriage

The Chief Justice Roberts and the Supreme Court majority betrayed democracy and the Constitution by saying the sponsors of Proposition 8 did not have legal standing to appeal after the ballot measure was struck down.

Both decisions against the majority of California voters were unconstitutional and unconscionable.

It didn't matter that Governor Jerry Brown and Attorney General Kamala Harris violated their oaths of office by refusing to defend Proposition 8, simply because they were against the will of the people, who passed the state constitutional amendment by a 52 percent vote.

San Francisco's tyranny by social intimidation and legal extortion has dealt fatal blows to our legal system and the traditional institution of marriage.

(Original letter)

Voters lose, gay federal judge and tyranny of the minority win

The Chief Justice Roberts and the Supreme Court majority betrayed democracy and the Constitution by saying the sponsors of Proposition 8 did not have legal standing to appeal after the ballot measure was struck down by Vaughn Walker, a gay a federal judge in San Francisco. Both decisions against the majority of California voters were unconstitutional and unconscionable.

It didn't matter that former Attorney General, now Governor Jerry Brown and Attorney General Kamala Harris violated their oaths of office by refusing to defend Proposition 8 simply because they were against the will of the people, who passed the state constitutional amendment by a 52 percent vote, prohibiting gay marriage.

Alas, the tyranny of San Francisco and the gay minority by social intimidation and legal extortion have dealt fatal blows to our legal system and the traditional institution of marriage, confirming the dangers of what is becoming a superficial society of moral decay, social aggression, political terrorism, selfish interests and extremes.

Los Angeles Times
Opinion L.A.
June 29, 2013

Re: Proposition 8 deserved a state defense
By Erwin Chemerinsky

Erwin Chemerinsky is correct. Proposition 8 deserved a state defense.

The Chief Justice Roberts and the Supreme Court majority betrayed democracy and the Constitution by saying the sponsors of Proposition 8 did not have legal standing to appeal after the ballot measure was struck down by a gay federal judge in San Francisco. Both decisions against the majority of California voters were unconstitutional and unconscionable.

It didn't matter that former Attorney General, now Governor Jerry Brown and Attorney General Kamala Harris violated their oaths of office by refusing to defend Proposition 8 simply because they and the federal judge had conflicts of interest against the will of the people, who passed the state constitutional amendment by a 52 percent vote, prohibiting gay marriage.

Alas, the tyranny of San Francisco and the gay minority by social intimidation and legal extortion have dealt fatal blows to our legal system and the traditional institution of marriage, confirming the dangers of what is becoming a superficial society of moral decay, social aggression, political terrorism, selfish interests and extremes.

San Diego Union-Tribune
June 12, 2013

Snowden guilty of treason

NSA leaker Edward Snowden seems to be motivated by government's massive intrusion on Americans' phone calls, emails, monitoring internet activity, and other communications. However, he has not explained alerting our enemies to America's communications security system, which is tantamount to treason.

More troubling at this point is Snowden's history of dropping out of high school and college, briefly being in and out of Army Special Forces, being a NSA security guard, a CIA employee, then going to NSA as an administrative analyst -- which calls into question why he was hired and trusted with security clearance.

Indeed, at this point with more releases of classified information to come, it is highly likely, the unstable Mr. Snowden is doing nothing more than gaining international fame for being infamous -- which is a condemnation of those who failed to screen out a potential traitor. There's nothing heroic about that.

San Bernardino Sun
June 7, 2013

Forest Service fire suppression unacceptable

The Santa Clarita 'Powerhouse Fire' would not have exploded to over 30,000 acres if the fire services had used 'Super Scoopers' and DC 10 air tankers for a first strike against the fire when it was small.

Indeed, Super Scoopers -- capable of dropping 2000 gallons of water in 12 seconds -- alone could have put out the fire since they could have used nearby Lake Hughes to draw from.

Surely, if Super Scoopers and DC 10 tankers had been used to make their massive water drops when the Camarillo fire and the Frasier Park fire first started, the fires would have been extinguished -- end of story. Indeed, if they were used on the Oak Hills fire before it crested the Southwest area of the Cajon Pass, the fire would not have spread any further.

Certainly, the U.S. Forest Service has a dismal record in fire fighting throughout the country, and certainly in California. If they had called in the super tankers on the fire that devastated the San Bernardino National Forest Lake Arrowhead area, and the Station Fire in the Angeles National Forest, the losses would have been minimal.

Public safety fire service nonfeasance, needlessly costing lives and property, is simply unconscionable and unacceptable.

Riverside Press-Enterprise
June 5, 2013

Boy Scouts take wrong trail in approving gay members
Scouts take wrong trail

I'm a Bronze Palm Eagle Scout and have been active as a Boy Scouts district executive committee member. I've also been married for 53 years with three children, and I'm retired after 41 years of service in law enforcement and the criminal justice system. I credit the scouts with giving me a moral core, sense of duty to God and country, and the foundation of being a good, self-reliant citizen ("Boy Scouts lifts its ban on openly gay youngsters," May 25).

However, I'm dismayed by BSA leadership giving in to gay extremists and politically correct liberals to OK gays as members.

The Washington Examiner
May 30, 2013

Holder is investigating himself again

Re: *"Justice investigating IRS targeting the Tea Party,"* May 15

From the time presidential candidate Barack Obama campaigned on fundamentally transforming America, we have seen steady growth of government regulations and spending accompanied by insurmountable debt -- all supported by the liberal state media. Years of liberal indoctrination by the education establishment have left most Americans clueless about the Obama administration's insidious machinations to undermine the Constitution, or the deep chilling effect they have had on his opposition, as evidenced by the IRS targeting conservatives and the Tea Party and the Justice Department targeting the Associated Press and Fox News reporters.

As usual, President Obama feigned outrage when it was exposed, then fired the IRS Commissioner and ordered his Attorney General Eric Holder to investigate, even though Holder had signed the order to investigate James Rosen, Fox's chief Washington correspondent, as a co-conspirator on a national security leak.

Just like Holder investigating the "Fast and Furious" Holder about his blatant abuse of power, this is a redundant gesture.

(original letter)

From the time presidential candidate Barack Obama campaigned on fundamentally transforming America, his presidential actions, diversions, distractions and deceptions tantamount to outright lies paved the way to accomplishing his liberal agenda -- beginning with ramming his national health care legislation through a complicit Democrat Congress.

Indeed, from then on it was steady government and regulatory growth, spending and insurmountable debt by leaps and bounds -- all supported by the liberal state media, who got President Obama elected and led him into a second term, but not before he lost the House of Representatives to Republicans backed by the spontaneously formed Tea Party in opposition to the president's health careless laws, spending and insurmountable debt.

No thanks to the liberal press and years of liberal indoctrination of students by the education establishment, most of America is clueless about President Obama and his administration's insidious machinations undermining the Constitution, and the deep freeze chilling effect he has on his opposition -- as evidenced by the IRS targeting the Tea Party, conservative groups and individuals -- and the Justice Department targeting Associated Press and Fox News reporters.

Of course, as usual, President Obama feigned outrage at the exposures, fired the IRS Commissioner, and ordered his Attorney General Eric Holder to review policies and investigate, even though Holder had signed the order to investigate FOX's Chief Washington Correspondent, James Rosen as a co-conspirator on a national security leak. Surely, Holder investigating "Fast and Furious" Holder and his blatant abuse of power is a redundant gesture.

Alas, lest we forget, it is President Obama's dictatorial regulations, legislative tyrannies, government growth and his gang of liberal Democrats that are limiting our free speech and liberties -- ruining our economy and our culture, not to mention risking our national security by toying with terrorism -- when it is much smaller limited constitutional government that we need to survive.

The New York Post
May 29, 2013

BSA's new policy on gays: Sizing up the fallout

The issue: Whether the Boy Scout's decision to accept gay youths but not adults undermines its ideals
(second of five letters)

As a Bronze Palm Eagle Scout, active as a BSA district executive committee member, married for 53 years with three children and retired from 41 years of service in law enforcement and the criminal justice system, I credit the BSA with giving me the moral core, duty to god and country and the foundation of being a good self-reliant American citizen.

However, I am deeply dismayed by BSA leadership giving-in to intimidation by gay extremists and the liberal politically correct to accept gays as members of the BSA.

Likewise, I am deeply concerned by the national trend of states to damage traditional marriage by accepting same-sex marriage -- and the federal government's refusal to defend the Defense of Marriage, which further undermines the strength of our social fabric.

Daily Press - Apple Valley Review
May 28, 2013

Obama's mounting articles of impeachment

It's already obvious that the 9/11 anniversary Benghazi, Libya terrorist attack costing the lives of our ambassador and three security personnel was the result of intentional malfeasance by President Obama and Secretary of State Clinton.

Worse, the deceitful cover-up is tantamount to giving aid and comfort to our Islamic jihadist terrorist enemy to further a re-election campaign and to protect Obama and Clinton at any cost.

Even worse, the ongoing Teflon provided by the ideology-driven liberal media to President Obama and presumptive 2016 nominee Hillary Clinton -- and the demonization of all opposition -- is an unconscionable abdication of public responsibility by the press.

It was bad enough that the President Obama's campaign promises supporting the passage of Obamacare were a pack of lies concealing the devastating costs and cuts in America's healthcare coverage -- in addition to the wasteful, useless spending of his enormous stimulus packages, economy-busting regulations, national debt expansion.

Now comes reports that as early as the 2010 passage of Obamacare, and during the re-election campaign, administrative tyranny was launched by President Obama's IRS against the Tea Party and other conservative opposition's tax exemption status -- in addition to the merciless demonizing of all opposition of any description. Indeed, even the New York Times criticized the administration's abusive IRS tactics against the Tea Party in a March 2012 editorial.

Subsequently, the president's sequester idea developed into selective pain from government cuts in FAA air traffic controllers and all manner of other unnecessary cuts designed to adversely affect the public -- placing blame on Republicans -- all intended to reclaim Democrat control of the House of Representatives in 2014.

Certainly, President Obama has made it painfully and abundantly clear that he has no problem defying Congress, ignoring the constraints of the Constitution, and the will of the people to do or get what he wants -- un-American as it may be.

Clearly, President Obama's costly ideology-driven executive orders, and administrative edicts and regulations amounting to tyrannical administrative abuse of power and cover-ups, along with patterns of lies and deceit, dereliction of duty against terrorism, border security -- and his failings in national and domestic security -- are stacking up as prospective articles of impeachment.

Lest we forget, it was House Republicans who moved ahead with hearings on the Watergate cover-up and articles of impeachment against former Republican president Nixon's abuse of power resulting in his resignation. Which begs the question: Where are the Democrats in the mounting evidence against President Obama and his captains of corruption?.

The problem is: President Obama will likely never be impeached and convicted because congressional Democrats and the liberal press are unlikely to let it happen -- and America will undoubtedly suffer the consequences.

Newsmax Magazine
June 2013 issue

Challenging DOMA

The Defense of Marriage Act was made federal law and California's Proposition 8 denied same-sex marriage. Proposition 8 was passed by voters. Neither law was defended by President Obama's U.S. attorney general or Gov. Jerry Brown's state attorney general -- simply because it is not politically correct. That is gross malfeasance ("Supreme Court Tries to Avoid Another Roe v. Wade," May).

America's culture can ill-afford to damage the right-to-life and the institution of marriage any further, yet both have come under assault from abortion and same-sex marriage extremists who intimidate all opposition with a vengeance. A free and healthy society that abdicates its responsibility to itself is surely doomed.

San Diego Union-Tribune
May 22, 2013

President Obama and the IRS scandal

Tea Party lawyer Dan Becker was correct in saying, "When you make is burdensome to speak, people don't speak. When you make it burdensome to associate, people don't associate." What the IRS has done is a blatant constitutional violation of First Amendment freedoms of speech and association -- and the right of the people to peaceably assemble, and to petition government for redress of grievances.

It's becoming painfully clear that President Obama's fingerprints are all over the IRS tyrannies against the Tea Party, conservative groups and individuals. Indeed, the president's demonization of the Tea Party and conservative groups set the tone for his IRS and captains of political intimidation to target and silence them.

[In early 2010, President Obama gave marching orders for Democrat activists to attack Tea Party and conservative groups, and for congressional Democrats to pressure the IRS to target them. Of course, the SEIU attacked Tea Party members and Democrat Senators, Chuck Schumer, Al Franken and others complied by pushing the IRS to take action.] (edited out)

Lest they forget, the Tea Party started as a spontaneous response to the government overreach and cost of Obamacareless, and objections to government spending and debt. As First Amendment as you can get.

(Original letter)

Tea Party lawyer Dan Becker was correct in saying, "When you make is burdensome to speak, people don't speak. When you make it burdensome to associate, people don't associate." What the IRS has done is a blatant constitutional violation of First Amendment freedoms of speech and association -- and the right of the people to peaceably assemble, and to petition government for redress of grievances.

It's becoming painfully clear that President Obama's fingerprints are all over the IRS tyrannies against the Tea Party, conservative groups and individuals. Indeed, the president's demonization of the Tea Party and conservative groups set the tone for his IRS and captains of political intimidation to target and silence them.

In early 2010, President Obama gave marching orders for Democrat activists to attack Tea Party and conservative groups, and for congressional Democrats to pressure the IRS to target them. Of course, the SEIU attacked Tea Party members and Democrat Senators, Chuck Schumer, Al Franken and others complied by pushing the IRS to take action.

President Obama's IRS hatchet man, acting Commissioner, Steve Miller contemptuously testified before a congressional House Committee, side-stepping questions and confirming nothing but feigned ignorance and Sarah Hall Ingram's position as executive in charge of the tax-exempt division, which in 2010 began targeting the Tea Party, conservative groups, evangelical and pro-Israel groups.

Unfortunately, Ingram -- who received unconscionable bonuses for her dirty work -- was recently promoted to serve as director of the IRS Obamacare program office, which will exert tax and penalty tyrannies forcing compliance with Mr. Obama's ideological crown jewel, which will further damage or reverse economic recovery.

Lest they forget, the Tea Party started as a spontaneous response to the government overreach and cost of Obamacareless, and objections to government spending and debt. As First Amendment as you can get.

San Diego Union-Tribune
May 14, 2013

Re: Benghazi cover-up beyond a doubt - editorial

In response to "Benghazi cover-up beyond a doubt" (Editorial, May 8): It's already obvious that the 9/11 anniversary Benghazi terrorist attack costing the lives of our ambassador and three security personnel was the result of intentional malfeasance by President Obama and Secretary of State Clinton.

Worse, the deceitful cover-up is tantamount to giving aid and comfort to our Islamic jihadist terrorist enemy to further a re-election campaign and to protect Obama and Clinton at any cost.

Even worse, the ongoing Teflon provided by the ideology-driven liberal media to President Obama and presumptive 2016 nominee Hillary Clinton -- and the demonization of all opposition -- is an unconscionable abdication of public responsibility by the press.

A notable exception is the exceptional objectivity and truth in journalism provided by The San Diego Union-Tribune.

San Diego Union-Tribune
April 30, 2013

Sequester a shell game?

Harassing airline passengers by furloughing air traffic controllers was just another day of Democrat gangster politics using selective sequester budget cuts, until it affected the gangsters themselves, who quickly reversed the furloughs.

Godfather President Obama proposed the sequestration so Democrats could use the leverage against Republicans to raise taxes and increase spending.

This first round didn't work, but there is more extortion to come, designed to have Democrats retake the House of Representatives in 2014. However, when they try to exempt themselves and their staff from the negative impact of ObamaCareLess, the outlook is questionable.

Lest we forget, when economy-busting ObamaCareLess was rammed through the Democrat Congress and signed by the Godfather, President Obama thought his legacy was set in stone. Alas, little does he and his gang of Democrats know, that the damage will likely be carved on their political graves -- at America's unnecessary expense.

San Bernardino Sun
April 30, 2013

Police are the nation's first line of defense

The carnage in Boston brought on by the radicalized Muslim brothers intensifies the clear and present danger of the long record of inhuman savages who would wipe out all but fundamentalist Muslim human life on the planet, particularly in America. They say we are the great Satan, where in reality, the devil-Satan is their fanatical belief in extreme Jihad.

Our news media's saturation coverage of the terrorist attack and the over-analysis that followed is just what the terrorists want. Fear and chaos, spawning more of the same.

There is no question that we must bring about major changes for the enhancement of our national and domestic security. Particularly on our borders and with our visa, immigration and refugee/asylum seekers. We can no longer stand the near unfettered flow of foreign gangsters, criminals and terrorists to our nation.

Surely, being politically correct simply doesn't work when it breeds predators, parasites and terrorism. As a former law enforcement officer, with 41 years of experience in the criminal justice system, I know that the police are without question, our first line of defense. The Boston bombing is a prime example.

San Diego Union-Tribune
April 24, 2013

Terror in America

The carnage in Boston brought on by the radicalized Muslim brothers intensifies the clear and present danger of the long record of inhuman savages who would wipe out all but fundamentalist Muslim human life on the planet, particularly in America. They say we are the great Satan, where in reality, the devil-Satan is their fanatical belief in extreme Jihad.

Our news media's saturation coverage of the terrorist attack and the over-analysis that followed is just what the terrorists want. Fear and chaos, spawning more of the same.

There is no question that we must bring about major changes for the enhancement of our national and domestic security. Particularly on our borders and with our visa, immigration and refugee/asylum seekers. We can no longer stand the near unfettered flow of foreign gangsters, criminals and terrorists to our nation.

Surely, being politically correct simply doesn't work when it breeds predators, parasites and terrorism. As a former law enforcement officer, with 41 years of experience in the criminal justice system, I know that the police are without question, our first line of defense. The Boston bombing is a prime example.

San Diego Union-Tribune
April 10, 2013

Time for bold GOP action

It's time for Republicans to take bold steps to stem the destructive Democrat tide continuing with the re-election of President Obama. Indeed, it's bad enough that the president got much of what he wanted in tax increases with no spending cuts. Though it further damages the economy, it's a drop in the bucket compared to Obama's grand plan to "fundamentally transform America" by edict, executive order and political bullying.

By transforming his Cabinet starting with the ideological appointments of "yes-men" -- Lew to Treasury, Hagel to Defense, Kerry to State, and Brennan to the C.I.A. (not a cabinet position) -- President Obama will make it painfully clear that he will sacrifice economic recovery, the middle class, foreign policy, and our national security to attain his world view that the United States must lose its status of first in military and economic world power, exceptionalism and freedom.

Worse, President Obama's reckless efforts are enhanced by decades of indoctrination by the national liberal media, Hollywood, unions and the education establishment left, which are largely responsible for his election and re-election, as evidenced by relentless attacks against America's work force, free enterprise, wealth, the fight against terrorism, religion, law enforcement, the criminal justice system, the Constitution and family. Not to mention his intention to reduce our national defenses, and disarm the American people.

Surely, Republicans must take decisive actions to hold the line against government growth and abuse of power, and to retain the House and regain the Senate in 2014 by convincing the electorate that the GOP is the only way out of the pain they feel from this Democrat-caused mess. Indeed, the deceitful, insidious Obama-Democrat agenda must be exposed for what it really is. Socialism by sucking the economy dry, and breaking the spirit of liberty.

Los Angeles Times
Opinion L.A.
April 9, 2013

Re: Margaret Thatcher, political revoluntionary by Patt Morrison

Thatcher and Reagan: Those were the days

Former British Prime Minister Margaret Thatcher's passing should serve as a prime reminder that she and former President Ronald Reagan ended the Cold War and rescued the U.K and the United States from the corrosive social, political and economic erosion caused by liberal government.

Alas, since then, liberal government, social, environmental and union extremists have taken a devastating toll on our country and our freedoms, which is also beset by legal predators who constantly inflate the cost of living and health care, along with dependency parasites conditioned by government to suck the life out of America.

Indeed, what a shame it is to see the condescending commentary in the media, and indoctrinated British young people dancing for joy over Thatcher's death. Little do they know that if it were not for leaders like Reagan and Thatcher stopping the march of world Communism, they would likely be crawling for survival as slaves of the state.

Long live the memories of Margaret Thatcher and Ronald Reagan. We need them again, now, more than ever....

San Bernardino Sun
April 4, 2013

Same-sex marriage camp intimidates society

When the Defense Of Marriage Act was made federal law, and California's Proposition 8 denying same-sex marriage was passed by voters and neither law is defended by President Obama's U.S. attorney general or Gov. Brown's state attorney general -- simply because it's not politically correct -- that is gross malfeasance. And when courts that do the same it is judicial misconduct.

It's bad enough that traditional marriage has long suffered from attacks by liberals, feminists, the media and the entertainment industry. But when the attacks fundamentally affect relationships, families -- and the security of society because of single-parent children -- it is unconscionable.

Indeed, America's culture can ill-afford to damage the right-to-life and the institution of marriage any further -- yet it has been under assault from abortion and same-sex marriage extremists who intimidate all opposition. Alas, a free and healthy society that abdicates its responsibility to itself is surely doomed.

Desert Dispatch - Daily Press
March 31, 2013

In spite of liberals

The Los Angeles Times, the New York Times and all the left-stream media are practicing the height of hypocrisy by hailing Wall Street stock market gains as a series of new highs, not because of what President Obama and the Democrat cartel in Congress did over the past 5 years with their socialist effort at fundamentally transforming America, but what free enterprise and Capitalism has done in spite of it.

Worse, the liberal media continues to paint false pictures of the improving economy and unemployment numbers supporting President Obama's clouded vision and corrosive government growth. Lest we forget, it was President Carter and President Clinton who forced affordable housing on Fannie Mae, Freddie Mac, banks and mortgage lenders creating a sea of unqualified buyers -- and, the consequences of economic collapse.

San Diego Union-Tribune
March 30, 2012
Letters: **Gay marriage**

Same-sex marriage activists intimidating society

When the Defense Of Marriage Act was made federal law, and California's Proposition 8 denying same-sex marriage was passed by voters and neither law is defended by President Obama's U.S. attorney general or Governor Brown's state attorney general -- simply because it's not politically correct -- that is gross malfeasance. And courts that do the same is judicial misconduct.

It's bad enough that traditional marriage has long suffered from attacks by liberals, feminists, the media and the entertainment industry. But when the attacks fundamentally affect relationships, families -- and the security of society because of single-parent children -- it is unconscionable.

Indeed, America's culture can ill-afford to damage the right-to-life and the institution of marriage any further -- yet it has been under assault from abortion and same-sex marriage extremists who intimidate all opposition with a vengeance. Alas, a free and healthy society that abdicates its responsibility to itself is surely doomed.

The Washington Examiner
March 25, 2013

America cannot survive creeping socialism

Re: "Ted Cruz amendments: Repeal Obamacare, Block Bloomberg-style soda bans." March 22.
Texas Sen. Ted Cruz represents our founders' vision of liberty, as opposed to President Obama's crusade to accelerate the tyranny of socialism.

From its founding, America's vision has been slowly compromised by the subtle tyrannies of socialism. The result: a malfunctioning two-party system, systemic government growth, failed socialized education, health care and welfare, extreme regulation and government spending, punishing taxes, unsustainable debt, and the loss of our freedoms.

(original letter sentence edited out) Socialism is tantamount to treason against the United States.

America will simply not survive without a return to our original principles.

San Diego Union-Tribune
March 24, 2013

Sen. Feinstein vs. Sen. Cruz in gun control debate: Feinstein loses - not the war

In a rancorous debate with Texas Sen. Cruz over her gun control legislation, California Sen. Feinstein said that she resented being lectured like a 6-year-old, and that while mayor of San Francisco, she visited crime scenes and saw dead people that had been shot.

Unfortunately, while mayor of San Francisco, Feinstein also damaged the police investigation of "Night Stalker" serial killer Richard Ramirez by giving out investigative details to the press, which enraged investigators and delayed his capture -- costing more lives.

Feinstein and other intrusive Democrats have a long history of sticking their unconstitutional political noses where they don't belong, like making our Mojave Desert off-limits to private development, and sticking government group homes in private single-family neighborhoods, raising crime and lowering property values.

Sen. Feinstein lost a battle but not the war against freedom. The dynamic-duo demons of federal and California state government will never give up -- unless we take the sword-slashing-liberty away from them: Being elected and re-elected.

NewsMax Magazine
April 2013 issue
March 23, 2013

Dividing America

President Obama invokes his liberal "creed" upon America with his second-term 2013 inauguration speech, marking the second half of the liberal Obama era.

He seriously diminishes the best interests of the American people ("President's Plan Divides the Nation," March).

Obama promised to fundamentally transform America, and that's exactly what his presidency has done.

San Diego Union-Tribune
March 23, 2013

Hollywood is hurting America

Hollywood taking dramatic or artistic license in fact-based or true stories such as Academy Award nominated movies, "Argo," Lincoln" and "Zero Dark Thirty," is one thing. However, it cannot be stretched to a facsimile or copy of the truth when the theme of the plot is altered or tainted by ideology. Indeed, it simply doesn't read the same when it promotes a liberal agenda.

Worse, American history revisionists such as Howard Zinn's book, "People's History of the United States," -- widely used in our education system of corrupted indoctrination -- and currently, Oliver Stone's book and film, "The Untold History of the United States," serve nothing more than the author's and artist's efforts to undermine the historical meaning of our noble culture.

Alas, Hollywood and liberal politicians' deceit in promoting socialism over capitalism, democracy and freedom is bad enough. But when children's stories such as "Snow White," "The Wizard of Oz" and "Jack and the Beanstalk" are warped by Hollywood into violent-action movie extremes, that is simply unconscionable.

Victor Valley Daily Press
March 21, 2013

Socialism and treason

Texas Senator Cruz testified that he represents our founders' vision of liberty, as opposed to President Obama's crusade to accelerate the tyranny of socialism.

From our founding, America had only one vision, which has been slowly compromised by the subtle tyrannies of socialism. The result: a malfunctioning two-party system, systemic government growth, failed socialized education, socialized health care, socialized welfare, extreme regulation and government spending, punishing taxes, unsustainable debt, and the loss of freedoms.

Socialism is tantamount to treason against the United States. America will simply not survive without a return to our original principles and the realized vision of true liberty.

CHAPTER 2

Unpublished Letters: 2013 - 2015

USA TODAY
January 26, 2015

Re: Obama ups ante on Alaska oil war

President Obama is waging war against coal, oil and much more

President Obama and his liberal Democrat culture have been waging war against America since his 2008 election. Clearly, the president's latest attack against oil by designating 1.5 million oil-rich acres in Alaska a wilderness area, and refusal to approve the Keystone Pipeline -- added to his EPA's crushing blows against the coal industry -- is painful proof of his campaign promise that our electric bills would necessarily "skyrocket," in favor of costly and unreliable renewable energy.

Indeed, we now know that when then Senator Obama boldly stated that he was going to fundamentally transform America -- by undermining our freedoms -- he meant it.

Certainly, President Obama and his Democrat Congress undermined our economic freedoms with his national healthcare, ObamaCareless Act, and the Dodd Frank finance legislation. Worse, Mr. Obama's foreign policy and feckless war against terrorism has put our nation at extreme risk, particularly by playing into the feigned negotiating hands of the world's largest state sponsor of terrorism,

Iran while they develop nuclear weapons and expand their influence throughout the Middle East – with little or no resistance.

Surely, President Obama blatantly lied in his 2015 State of the Union speech when he said that he had no more campaigns to run, when in fact he has never stopped campaigning, and won't stop during his last two years in office. The question is, how much more damage will he inflict upon us? Fortunately, Congress is now controlled by Republicans, albeit subject to Mr. Obama's veto. Hopefully, the presidency will go to a Republican in 2016 instead of incompetent Hillary Clinton – a poor choice for the first woman president – as it sadly was for the first black president.

Alas, America is steeped in uncertainty from being assaulted by big government, abuse of power, regulations taxation and debt – and battered by the failures of good intentions. Hopefully, the Republican Party will nominate Gov. Mitt Romney again, with an articulate running-mate such as Sen. Rubio or Gov. Huckabee. He clearly learned from his 2012 campaign mistakes, he is an honest man with high integrity, extensive executive experience, and he will be strong for our society, our economy and our national security.

Certainly, our freedoms, our future, our security and democracy are in the hands of our fellow voters – a voter nation of fools -- until we took control of the House in 2010, slipped back to President Obama in 2012 – then took control of the Senate in 2014. We will need Romney in 2016, to pick up the pieces, recover and move on to liberty and prosperity.

The Wall Street Journal
January 22, 2015

Re: Obama, Congress clash on Iran – Front Page

Netanyahu should address Congress: Israel imperiled by Iran nukes

House Speaker John Boehner did the right thing by inviting Israeli Prime Minister Benjamin Netanyahu to address a joint session of Congress. Indeed, President Obama's lengthy negotiations with devious Iran are simply a foolish exercise in futility against Iran's continued pursuit of developing nuclear weapons.

Clearly, it is well-known and understood that Iran is on a declared mission to eliminate Israel with a nuclear attack, which has been frequently pointed out by Prime Minister Netanyahu. And clearly, Iran intends to attack the United States, dominate the Middle East and carry on an intensified Jihad against the West and all non-believers.

Though President Obama rattles (rubber) swords of all options against Iran's deadly pursuit, he dangerously insists on diplomatic negotiations without increasing economic sanctions, which are the only things that work against Iran. Discouraging Congress from increasing sanctions, and Israel from taking any pre-emptive military action is ludicrous.

Attention, President Obama: Coupled with the growing insanity of ISIS, Islamic extremists are on a deadly course to crush Israel, America and the West. Working against Israel's survival, endangering our country and inviting WW III with shallow diplomatic delays is not an option.

Lest we forget, former president Bill Clinton disliked Prime Minister Netanyahu, which cost him re-election and increased the threat to our national security. The same holds true with Mr. Obama, both of which smack of being anti-Israel, our only real ally in the Middle East, stupid!

The Wall Street Journal
January 20, 2015

First black and first woman presidents

The 2008 election of Barack Obama as the first black president was hailed by Democrats, the fawning media and others. However, voters can't say they were not forewarned about Obama's socialist past and intentions to "fundamentally transform America," which he has done with an ideological vengeance.

Indeed, with 6 years into Obama's presidency -- highlighted by his 2015 State of the Union taxation speech – he has made it painfully clear that his intentions and abuse of executive power pursuing socialism are clearly un-American, causing severe damage to the nation's security, economy, and the people.

Certainly, Barack Obama was one of, if not the worst choices for the first black president. Hopefully, voters will not make the same mistake with the first woman president, which could be Democrat front-runner, Hillary Clinton. Granted, voters might long to return to the reduction in government and the prosperity of Bill Clinton's presidency of the 90's – thanks to Newt Gingrich's Congress and the Contract with America.

Lest we forget, it was President Clinton who caused the 2007-2008 economic housing and financial crash with his blind pursuit of affordable housing. And it was First Lady, Hillary Clinton who secretly attempted to impose national health care on the country – not to mention firing the White House Travel Office staff and replacing them with her Hollywood friends.

Coupled with her poor performances as a U.S. Senator and Secretary of State, that would certainly make her one of, if not the worst choice to be the first woman president. Indeed, two strike-outs against America.

Los Angeles Times
January 18, 2015

Obama and Cameron accelerate Iran nukes

In a joint White House press conference, backed by British Prime minister David Cameron, President Obama vehemently discouraged Congress from increasing sanctions against Iran to further his hapless diplomatic efforts to prevent Iran from continuing its pursuit of nuclear weapons.

However, it has always been known and understood that Iran will negotiate in bad faith to gain time to do what they want, regardless of the consequences, in their history of extreme hatred of Israel, Jews, the United States and the West.

Therefore, President Obama's reckless behavior, ignoring the success of economic sanctions -- and his opposition to Israel making pre-emptive strikes to prevent Iran from completing their ongoing development of nuclear weapons – will surely result in Israel taking defensive action when necessary.

Indeed, the worst case scenario would be for Iran to obtain the nukes, use them against Israel -- which would result in activating Israel's missile defense system and a retaliatory nuclear strikes against Iran, nuclear war and accelerate WW III – which is already underway by the rapid growth of fanatic Islamic terrorists.

Washington Post
January 17, 2015

Obama's free college indoctrination

President Obama's national program for free community college tuition, like Obamacare and any government program, is not free. Indeed, it costs local, state and federal taxpayers and comes with other strings attached: More curriculum control of the socialism indoctrination of young people, thus more Democrat voters.

Coupled with the president's unconscionable "Common Core" standards of the indoctrination of elementary and secondary students, government control of student loans -- and the deeply imbedded indoctrination of 4-year colleges, universities and graduate students – America's miseducation system will surely become completely un-American, with few exceptions.

Clearly, the only solution to this dangerous and corrosive social, political and economic disease is to privatize education – before it's too late. In a world wrought with terrorism, our freedoms and our survival are at stake….

USA TODAY
January 16, 2015

Re: No Oscar diversity
Front Page

President Obama taking on Hollywood

Selma's nomination for Best Picture notwithstanding, USA TODAY, the Los Angeles Times and other liberal media are supporting President Obama's tacit dissatisfaction with Hollywood's Academy Awards for failure to include black actors, directors, writers and others in this year's major Oscar nominations, which resulted in the president's black race relations counselor and chief racist extortionist, Al Sharpton to call a summit meeting with Hollywood and demand answers.

Indeed, it doesn't matter that an abundance of black films were made and released, and that blacks and women have been over-represented in films, television programs and commercials in the Obama era. Clearly, all that matters is that the Academy of Motion Picture Arts and Sciences voters are 94% white and 77% male, who are not towing the line of black superiority in the upper class of untouchable sacred cows regardless of character, talent and ability.

Alas, in marked contrast to under-represented Latinos, a sad state of affairs. Particularly, with the severe overall lack of quality Hollywood entertainment.

Wall Street Journal
December 20, 2014

Re: **The Cuban regime is a defeated foe**
By Peggy Noonan

Peggy Noonan is wrong. The Cuban regime is not a defeated foe. They now have President Obama breathing new life into the Communist state sponsor of terrorism. Senator Rubio is correct: President Obama betrays America for Castro

President Obama's reckless move to normalize relations with Cuba comes as no surprise. Indeed, considering the prisoner exchange, his next move will probably be to clear out Guantanamo and give it back to the Communist country. Either way, together with granting amnesty for 5-20 million illegal immigrants and leaving our border open to more – including criminals and terrorists -- Mr. Obama is increasing the threat to our country.

Coupled with the president's disastrous record of allowing terrorism to expand in power throughout the Middle East with ISIS, al-Qaeda and the Muslim Brotherhood -- surrendering to the Taliban, Russia's aggression, being negative toward Israel, and ignoring Iran's deceit to create nuclear weapons -- President Obama is surely toying with terrorism and turning an intentional blind eye to our nation's overall national security.

Certainly, making deals with the devil comes easy to President Obama. Who's next, North Korea? With just over two years left in his second term, the president is accelerating his unconscionable agenda to divide and weaken America – and to punish our nation for what he perceives as past crimes – regardless of the consequences. Hopefully, with a Republican Congress and Republican elected president in 2016, the tide will turn back to a safer, more prosperous and stable America as it was meant to be.

USA TODAY
December 19, 2014

Sony gets it wrong, like most of Hollywood

Sony's movie, "The Interview," a stupid comedy depicting the attempt assassination of North Korea's leader is not funny, but comes a no surprise. Indeed, the only surprise was North Korea's hacker attack on Sony and the threats against airing the movie that resulted in Sony's surrender.

It's unconscionable enough that liberal Democrats and news media constantly compromise CIA and special operations, exacerbated by President Obama's surrender of America's national security in his half-hearted war on terror -- and his latest betrayal: diplomatic relations with Castro's Communist Cuba.

Hollywood's greedy arrogance simply makes it worse by depicting government operations and the CIA dancing with danger and toying with terrorism, which is widespread in movies and television series, such as Showtime's "Homeland," HBO's "Newsroom," CBS's "NCIS" series, and NBC's "Blacklist" and "Madam Secretary," followed by "State of Affairs."

Wall Street Journal
December 18, 2014

Senator Rubio is correct: President Obama betrays America for Castro

President Obama's reckless move to normalize relations with Cuba comes as no surprise. Indeed, considering the prisoner exchange, his next move will probably be to clear out Guantanamo and give it back to the Communist country. Either way, together with granting amnesty for 5-20 million illegal immigrants and leaving our border open to more – including criminals and terrorists -- Mr. Obama is increasing the threat to our country.

Coupled with the president's disastrous record of allowing terrorism to expand in power throughout the Middle East with ISIS, al-Qaeda and the Muslim Brotherhood -- surrendering to the Taliban, Russia's aggression, being negative toward Israel, and ignoring Iran's deceit to create nuclear weapons -- President Obama is surely toying with terrorism and turning an intentional blind eye to our nation's overall national security.

USA TODAY
December 14, 2014

Race relations in America

After decades of progress, race relations are obviously worse since President Obama was elected and became an imperial president, to the extent of giving African-Americans an arrogant superiority complex and/or being treated as sacred cows in the Obama era. Indeed, Hollywood and advertisers have responded by over-representing blacks in films, television and commercials.

Worse, racial protests, demonstrations, rioting, arson and looting have been exacerbated by President Obama, his aggressively radical race counselor, Al Sharpton, indoctrinated college students and the complicit news media -- touched off by the Travon Martin case -- then magnified by the Michael Brown and Eric Garner death cases at the hands of police -- who were not indicted by local grand juries.

Race relations will certainly deteriorate even further as the protests continue and grow throughout the country, invading streets, highways and freeways, blocking traffic and endangering the public – even blocking Christmas shoppers in stores and malls. President Obama should step-up to improve race relations as a major part of his legacy. If not, the insanity goes on, unabated......

Lest we forget, the police are our first line of defense in neighborhoods, communities and cities against criminals and terrorists.

Washington Times
December 10, 2014

The Ferguson Al Sharpton/Obama – news media effect

As a former deputy sheriff and county grand jury member with 43 years of experience in law enforcement and the criminal justice system dating back to 1960, I personally witnessed race relations with the police from the 1965 Watts Riots in Los Angeles – and the serious damage done by the counter-culture revolution -- through the turn of the century. Though we have come a long way since my first experiences, there is still room for improvement on both sides.

As for the present conflict that began in Ferguson, Missouri with the shooting death of Michael Brown by a white police officer and escalated throughout the country, it's one thing for people to peacefully march and protest in Los Angeles and San Diego. They are legally within their rights to do so, and the Los Angeles Police Department has reacted with commendable cooperation and restraint to protect those rights.

However, when those people turn to breaking the law by laying down in the street, blocking the roadways and intersections, then escalate that to blocking busy freeways and shopping malls – particularly when law-abiding people are going about their business and traveling to be with friends and relatives to celebrate the holiday season – that is way beyond civil disobedience.

Indeed, their shameless and outrageous behavior does nothing but turn people against what they are protesting for, and they should be prosecuted fully for their crimes – no less than opportunistic rioters, looters and arsonists who do have done serious damage to the innocent in Ferguson and St. Louis.

Surely, the obsessive lead, "White officer shot and killed unarmed black teen," by news media -- exacerbated racial hatred already stoked by extreme race activist Al Sharpton and others -- which resulted in violent demonstrations, arson and looting in Ferguson Missouri after the incident – and again -- after the grand jury found insufficient evidence to indict officer Darren Wilson for the death of Michael Brown is unconscionable.

This is an irresponsible media shame that does more to worsen race relations than to do what they should to improve them. Indeed, the same thing happened with the Travon Martin case involving an Hispanic/white neighborhood watch member who killed a black teen in self-defense. certainly, the media and protesters should be reminded that Michael Brown was not unarmed. He was armed with his aggression, size and strength -- and he used it.

Alas, a national movement of African-Americans against the police, escalated by race-baiters, agitators and extortionists, liberal indoctrinated college students, and the NAACP – perpetuated by the media and the Obama/Holder civil rights violation investigation -- does more to harm race relations that to help them. Indeed, a civil rights prosecution against Officer Wilson would be criminal persecution.

Sadly, Officer Wilson resigned from the Ferguson Police Department without severance pay because of threats against him, his family and the department. Indeed, he did the right thing, even though the threats against him will persist. Lest we forget, the police are the first line of defense against criminals, terrorists and invasion, who have sworn to risk their lives to protect all of us.

USA TODAY
December 7, 2014

Movement against police deeply troubling

Take it from a former law enforcement officer, public defender investigator and county grand jury member with 43 years of experience in the criminal justice system since the counter-culture movement of 1960's: The national movement against our police smacks of Saul Alinsky's book, Rules for Radicals. Creating chaos is what terrorists, socialists and communists do to gain control.

Indeed, the racial exploitation being conducted by President Obama, Attorney General Holder, the SEIU, George Soros and New York Mayor de Blasio is deeply troubling and divisive. Lest we forget, the police are the first line of defense in America. The military are the deep defense of our nation, which is being micromanaged by the president to weaken it. We should support our police and military, and reject those who would take away our liberty.

Washington Post
December 2, 2014

President Obama's false promises and abuse of power

President Obama has proven that his presidency is based upon false campaign promises, manipulation, lies, deceit and the abuse of executive power. Clearly, the only campaign promise he kept was the fundamental transformation of America, which he has turned into a national nightmare.

Indeed, when Mr. Obama took office in the midst of a falling economy – with Democrat Congress – he added the first of an annual trillion dollars to the national debt (which just surpassed $18 trillion), established the economy-crushing Affordable Care Act of national health care, began a constant process anti-financial legislation and federal regulations, declared war against coal energy -- began a crusade for costly, unreliable green energy -- and embarked on the systematic deterioration of our domestic and national security.

As if that wasn't enough damage, President Obama invited mass illegal border crossings and bypassed Congress and unconstitutionally granted costly amnesty to 6 million illegal immigrants. And now, he has interjected his administration into the killing of a black (adult) 18-year-old teen by a white Ferguson, Missouri police officer with a civil rights investigation, while being counseled by racial radical Al Sharpton, and is holding court on African-American community/police relations.

Alas, our beleaguered nation will have to endure this president's quest for a legacy with narcissistic machinations for his remaining two years in office.

USA TODAY
November 22, 2014

Emperor Obama

President Obama's unconstitutional executive order of amnesty for 5 million illegal immigrants, and the $billions it will cost, comes as no surprise.

Mr. Obama's deceitful actions have already exacted a heavy toll upon America since he took office and crowned himself emperor, including Obamacare, punishing regulations, energy, finance, taxation, debt, foreign policy, domestic and national security, and our freedoms.

Indeed, his legacy will undoubtedly be replete with abuse of power until his last day in office. Unfortunately, Californians will still be under the tyranny of King Brown and his minions in the Legislature for two years beyond that. Question is, when will voters feel enough pain to vote for freedom?

Wall Street Journal
November 11, 2014

Internet.gov?

It's bad enough that President Obama's pending executive order on immigration policy will be Obamagrationcareless, not so different from Obamacareless. Talk about abuse of power, the next edict on his agenda is so-called Internet Neutrality, which would be nothing less than the tyranny of Internet.gov. Clearly, (King) Obama has been monarchial with nearly everything he's done since his election. Indeed, the more resistance there is, the more sanctimonious liberal abuse of power there will be. Unfortunately, sanctimonious Democrats have become a dreadful way of life in Washington and throughout the states, dictating their abusive policies against our freedoms, our society, our economy, and our domestic and national security. Period,

Los Angeles Times
October 26, 2014

Governor Brown's bad propositions 1, 2 and 47

It's bad enough that Governor Brown and the Democrat Legislature have hustled voters and sold-out California to environmental zealots, social engineers and the teacher unions with economy-busting regulations, the costly miseducation of our children, AB 32's cap-and-tax business and job killer, and Proposition 30's tax lies. Alas, it seems that there is no end to unconstitutional government's abuse of power in what has become the fool's gold state, leaving taxpayers $68 billion in bond debt to run Brown's fraudulent toy bullet train that most taxpayers will never use.

Indeed, Brown's current round of deceitful Propositions will do nothing but do more harm to our economy and security when administered by self-serving political fraud. Propositions 1 and 2 are being sold to store water in the drought, and provide emergency funds for fire fighting. In reality, the drought has been exacerbated by an activist federal court decision to cut 30 percent of water from the property owner-funded California Water Project to protect Delta Smelt and allow millions of acre-feet of water to flow into the ocean -- depriving Central and Southern California farmers and people of water -- While Brown's administration does nothing to prevent it.

Adding dangerous insult to economic injury, Brown's AB 109 prison disaster dumps thousands of felony prisoners on county jails, most of whom are illegal alien criminals welcomed to California by Democrats and President Obama, along with millions of illegal aliens who are sucking $billions of taxpayer dollars from government healthcare and welfare services along with education to pay for potential voters. Now, Brown wants voters to pass Proposition 47 to exacerbate the problem with prisoners released to prey on the people.

Sadly, Governor Brown, Attorney General Kamala Harris and Democrat legislators will surely be re-elected by foolish voters bent on social, political and economic suicide, not to mention Brown and Harris' dereliction of duty for refusing to defend Proposition 8 and traditional marriage.

New York Times
October 25, 2014

Al Sharpton's brand of injustice

Al Sharpton is in essence a one-man lynch mob calling for Ferguson police officer Darren Wilson to be strung-up to the nearest tree. Sharpton incited people into a lynch mob from the first day he spewed his brand of racism in Ferguson. Indeed, Sharpton cannot bothered with facts when he has already made up his mind, regardless of the justice system. He's done it before, and he's doing it again. Worse, Sharpton's brand of no justice, no peace, makes him a dangerous man, seriously damaging to racial relations and our fragile society. Alas, President Obama and Attorney General Eric Holder seeking

Sharpton's counsel in this case and giving him credibility is simply unconscionable.

Washington Post
October 17, 2014

ISIS, Iran, Russia and Ebola

Because of President Obama's weakness, incompetence and hands-off policy against rapidly growing threats to our national security from ISIS, Iran, Russian aggression, illegal alien criminals crossing our Southern border, and now Ebola. Indeed, endless tribal wars in the Middle East have escalated, and the endless ideological war waged by Russia against America and Eastern European democracies with no force standing in their way -- least of all from our president.

President Obama will not commit ground troops to fight ISIS, but he sent 3000 troops to Liberia to fight Ebola by building medical facilities and now to assist in handling body fluid samples of suspected Ebola patients. Our troops choose to fight for their country and are expected to defend America and threats to our national security. The troops Mr. Obama sent to Liberia and the dangers of being exposed to Ebola had no choice.

Alas, the deadly Ebola virus had never infected the United States until President Obama's politically correct policies allowed it to happen. In Mr. Obama's zeal to help Liberia and Africa at any cost, he failed to ban West African travel to America, which allowed a Liberian national to lie about his exposure to Ebola and reach our country infected with virus, thus infecting at least two others at a Dallas hospital.

Worse, because of our inept president, America is exposed to more deadly terrorist attacks on our homeland, more exposure to Ebola, and a dim outlook for our decaying economy -- leaving us nearly helpless for Mr. Obama's remaining two years in office. Clearly, our only hope is for Republicans to take over the Senate this year and a Republican president in 2016.

Los Angeles Times
October 9, 2014

Gay marriage is wrong

The legal battle for and against gay marriage, traditional marriage and families has come to a tragic end at the hands of the tyranny of feminists, gay activists and the federal courts who have abdicated their constitutional responsibility.

The courts have failed to uphold states' constitutional rights in favor of fictitious gay rights and adoptions of innocent children who have no choice. And the undermining of America's morals, values and the sanctity of life and marriage goes on, unabated.

Hopefully, voters will see the light and do the right thing to save themselves from corrosive liberal ideology and big intrusive government before it's too late.

Wall Street Journal
October 4, 2014

Government is cooking the employment books.

It's way past time for the media to make headlines focusing on government deceit in unemployment numbers. Indeed, the truth is that the unemployment rate did not drop to 5.9%. That's a political lie. The truth is the unemployment rateis more than 11%, even as much as 15%. And wages are stagnant.

Government cooking the books is obvious. They say that employment picked up over 200,000 jobs, but they don't say that the labor force fell again by 97,000 people who have given up looking for work. They are unemployed by either early retirement, going on food stamps and welfare, or just stopped looking. In other words, the labor participation rate fell again to 62%. And there are growing hundreds of thousands of people who are under-employed or part-time.

Clearly, the only growth going on in America is too much government, taxes, rules, regulations, waste, fraud, lies, deceit and abuse of power. It's simply an unconstitutional, unconscionable disgrace and must be turned around to constitutional limited government, more freedom, and no more government than we absolutely need.

USA TODAY
September 24, 2014

Obama's UN Speech legacy

President Obama's speech to the United Nations confirms that he believes he is the world healer, while his domestic policy is ruining our economy and our freedoms. Indeed, Mr. Obama is betraying our national security while he fights the fires of terrorism with sticks, stones and a garden hose to finish his time in office. That will likely be the curse of President Obama's legacy. God help America.

Los Angeles Times
September 15, 2014

California steeped in decline

Clearly, California is steeped in decline from being undermined by a corrosive Democrat political ideology occupying Sacramento, activist courts, extreme liberals, radical environmentalists; mismanaged water resources; anti-business taxes and onerous regulations; failing public education exacerbated by the selfish interests power of teacher unions; a failed penal system putting the population at extreme risk; punishing personal and property taxes -- and a deceitful, tyrannical government bent on sucking the life out of the state and the people. Hopefully, California voters will wise-up to the fraud and stop the bleeding. Otherwise, California will certainly be headed for voter-assisted social, political and economic suicide....

Los Angeles Times
September 3, 2014

Dr. Hansen, Al Gore and President Obama: Global Warming/ Climate Change

California's current 100-year drought-scare as a "a threat to civilization" fits the profile of insidious environmental extremists and global warming/climate change alarmists, Dr. James E. Hansen, Al Gore's "Inconvenient Truth" and President Obama's climate action plan, which threaten serious damage to our country and the American people.

Indeed, the "Chicken-little sky is falling" began its urgency with NASA climate scientist, Dr. Hansen's work on human-emissions of greenhouse gases and rising temperatures in the 1970's culminating in his declaration before a Congressional committee in 1988 that human-induced global warming had begun -- as did Hansen's career of being the chief perpetrator of global warming fraud on the planet.

Dr. Hansen' crusade was followed by the scurrilous politics of former vice-president Al Gore's lucrative campaign against global warming with his 1992 book, *"Earth in the Balance,"* and his 2006 Academy Award-winning global warming alarmist blockbuster, *"An Inconvenient Truth."*

Now comes President Obama, with his Climate Change Action Plan to cut carbon emissions and fulfill the environmental obsession over global warming - conveniently changed to climate change because of periods of global cooling -- by escalating the attacks on coal, fossil fuels and industrial carbon emissions with punishing regulations and taxation -- as is being done by California Governor Jerry Brown with the AB-32 carbon taxes, all of which will break the back of our economy.

Alas, only voters can save us from economic extinction, that is, if they wise-up before it's too late.

USA TODAY
August 20, 2014

American sacred cows? No.

Investigative reporting has revealed there is strong evidence that there has been an overreaction and a rush to judgment in the police shooting death of Michael Brown in Missouri, exacerbated by media saturation, outside hateful activists, looting, violence, President Obama and Attorney General Eric Holder.

At this point there is evidence -- considering Brown's enormous size, a video of him committing a strong-arm robbery indicating he is a deadly weapon who assaulted the officer attempting to get the officer's weapon -- that may very well lead to a justified self-defense shooting. Unfortunately, with the Missouri governor calling for a vigorous prosecution of the officer, and an immediate grand jury indictment, there is doubt that true justice will prevail. Clearly, this unnecessary situation of racial hysteria over a white officer shooting a black man is a sad commentary on selfish political interests and the decline of our society.

Contrary to popular liberal belief, feminists, African Americans, gays and lesbians are not social untouchables. Indeed, American freedom and liberty cannot be compromised by sacred cows, or big, aggressive government resulting in damage to families and relationships, self-reliance, traditional marriage, and an overall loss of freedoms.

Los Angeles Times
August 10, 2014

Re: **Why are we back in Iraq?**
L.A. Times editorial

The L.A. Times' continued position against air attacks against ISIS is irresponsible press, particularly, when our national security is at stake.

Indeed, it is deeply troubling that the news media did nothing to press the president to take immediate action against ISIS when they formed in Syria and invaded Iraq to establish an extreme Islamic state to make war against America and the West. Indeed, much worse than Osama bin Laden's stronghold in Afghanistan to launch the September 11, 2001 attack against the United States. Surely, President Obama's current action in northern Iraq comes with too little, too late

When the murderous intentions of ISIS were made deadly clear in their invasion of northern Iraq, it was painfully evident that the ISIS army of terrorists was committing genocide against Christians and non-conforming Muslims. And the body count of thousands continues, unabated.

President Obama could have easily stopped the invasion when it began with sustained airstrikes against the marching horde of ISIS militants, intense intelligence, and without putting American troops on the ground. But he didn't, and there are now 40,000 innocent people trapped on a mountain top dying from lack of food, water and shelter -- surrounded by ISIS.

Only now, in response to a worldwide outcry for assistance, President Obama made humanitarian aid air drops to the people on the mountain, supported by necessary air strikes. Better late than never doesn't cut it, Mr. President. Not when ISIS is so firmly entrenched -- with seized U.S. military weapons and equipment left by the Iraqi army -- and advancing against our ally, the Kurds, abandoned by our president.

Worse, ISIS is a known direct threat to the United States and our homeland. That threat must be stopped and eliminated. Coupled with the growing threat of al-Qaeda and all their affiliates, the Jihad fanatics are a threat to all faiths and people in the world and they must be neutralized, along with Iran and North Korea

Wall Street journal
August 6, 2014

Commander-in-Chief Obama was in Africa promoting business and aid when Major General Harold J. Greene was assassinated by an Afghan soldier, who shot the general four times in the back.

President Obama said nothing about it -- or the young girls held hostage by African terrorists -- and is just getting around to informally questioning deserter and traitor Sgt. Bergdahl who was traded for 5 major terrorists from GITMO.

Alas, it all amounts to a Dereliction of duty, incompetence and -- coupled with terrorism gone wild in the Ukraine, Iraq, Libya and Israel, and failure in deterring Iran's terrorist state and nuclear weapon ambitions -- a leaderless disgrace of American foreign policy and national security weakness.

Washington Post
July 22, 2014

Israel's last stand - and ours

President Obama's lack of support for Israel, ignoring the aggression of Hamas -- his feckless nuclear weapon negotiations with Iran, his weakness against Russia's aggression in the Ukraine -- and his lack of our border security have signaled his abandoning our national security and his failures in a world of tyrants and terrorists.

Iran-backed Hamas's relentless attacks against Israel have resulted in Israel defending itself by any means necessary including an all-out defensive into Gaza. Israel has an absolute right to defend itself and their historical homeland, including attacks on Iran's nuclear weapon facilities if necessary. Israel is a small Democratic island of 5 million Jews -- America's only ally -- in a sea of 300 million Muslims.

Syrian ISIS terrorists have conquered northern Iraq and they are attacking Christians, telling them to convert, pay a tax or die, resulting in Christians fleeing to Kurdish territory to escape the deadly persecution. Iran, al-Qaida and all Jihadist Muslims are on a mission to destroy Israel, America and the West, eliminate Jews, Christians and all who do not convert. Indeed, it's an unholy Jihad to rule the planet.

Unfortunately, President Obama's reduction of our nuclear weapons and our military opens the door to all of our enemies. Surely, the American people cannot allow that to continue, and it must be turned around in the 2014 and 2016 elections. We must stand with

Israel and our allies against all enemies, foreign and domestic with maximum strength as we always have -- or suffer the consequences. Freedom is at stake......

Washington Times
July 21, 2014

President Obama's legacy: a grim threat to our national security

By the time President Obama leaves office, his record will undoubtedly reflect that America's national security was seriously diminished. Indeed, it's bad enough that our country has been leaderless in foreign policy during Obama's presidency, whereas his domestic policy has subjected the people to overreaching regulations and the blatant abuse of unconstitutional authority damaging our economy and our freedoms.

However, our national security being threatened by the president ignoring the clear and present danger of Iran's nuclear weapon development -- the Arab Spring turning into destabilizing the Middle East with the spread of al-Qaida and related terrorist groups into Egypt, Libya, Syria, Iraq and other Muslim countries -- and Russia's aggression in Ukraine, while drastically reducing our military, our nuclear weapons and our defense missiles in Europe and Turkey -- is a clear and present danger to our national security and the world.

Adding insult to injury, President Obama is extending the nuclear weapons negotiations with Iran, until after the November elections, and releasing nearly $3 billion of Iran's frozen assets -- which they will surely use to speed up their nuclear weapon development -- while the president's lies, distractions, cover-ups, open-border policy, and perpetual political fundraising goes on and on, unabated.

Lest we forget, Iran is the most dangerous state sponsor of terrorism, including creation and support of Hamas and their never-ending attack on Israel in furtherance of Iran's dedication to the total destruction of Israel -- likely with nuclear weapons. Alas, most would likely agree that the future looks grim. Very grim.

Los Angeles Times
July 17, 2014

Re: **Shutting down death row** - editorial

California: What death penalty?

The Los Angeles Times -- a federal judge ruling lethal injection unconstitutional -- and the State of California's de facto abolition of the death penalty comes as no surprise, even though the voters of California have made it clear that they want the death penalty.

Orange County Federal Judge Cormac J. Carney was correct in ruling that California's execution system of extraordinary delays render the death penalty unpredictable, arbitrary and useless as retribution or deterrent -- thus in violation of the 8th Amendment's prohibition of cruel and unusual punishment.

It's bad enough that a Northern California federal judge incorrectly ruled that California's lethal injection system was cruel and unusual punishment even though it is used in many states and is the most humane way of administering the death penalty.

Surely, the will of the people should prevail regarding the death penalty, not the will of un-American Civil Liberties Union and others who could care less about the victims and families of horrendous murders who should be put to death.

As a Southern Californian retired from 41 years working in the criminal justice system, I've witnessed California's unconscionable decline in the administration of justice, unnecessarily making the people much less safe and secure against violent crime. That's injustice!

It is well known and understood that the death penalty is a deterrent against murder. California should follow the State of Texas in their administration of the death penalty: after a reasonable time for appeals, the death penalty is carried out as it should be. That's justice!

Washington Post
July 2, 2014

Imperial president vs. America

President Obama's executive action allowing a flood of 50,000 illegal alien children, parents and criminals -- and growing daily -- to remain in America by spreading them around to Border Patrol stations across the country for distribution to family members and into local communities is the latest blatant imperial action against our domestic and national security.

Clearly, it's bad enough that President Obama's imperial actions with Obamacare, against finance, the EPA cap and trade, and against energy will deal fatal blows to our economy.

However, imposing the unabated flow of illegal aliens upon communities such as Murrieta, California, others around the state and Arizona, amounts to imposed danger and a constant heavy impact on taxes paid by American citizens to cover their housing, education, healthcare and welfare -- in growing $billions of dollars we cannot afford -- is unconscionable.

Indeed, President Obama shamelessly uses arranged crisis to pursue his immigration reform agenda, without securing the border as is should be with fences, walls and establishing a militarized zone to stop the invasion of illegal aliens, drugs and crime.

Coupled with President Obama's dereliction of duty for failing to repel al-Qaida and ISIS from developing their border crossing attacks from Syria and Jordon into northern Iraq to establish their fanatical terrorist state and staging area to attack America and the West with their American and European terrorist members -- the clear and present danger to our country is unacceptable.

Certainly, America must stand up against Obama's imperialism, and the Supreme Court must step up their control of this out-of-control president early in their next term -- before it's too late....

Wall Street Journal
June 20, 2014

Obama abandons Iraq, and more

President Obama stood by while the Arab Spring turned into the rise of al-Qaida, the Muslim Brotherhood, ISIS, and other terrorist groups spreading Jihad throughout the Middle East, North Africa and Africa unabated.

The results have been the expansion of Muslims killing Muslims, now starkly manifested by the brutal ISIS invasion of northern Iraq to form the radical Islamic state of Syria and Iraq -- while Iran increases its hold on southern Iran and presses on with developing nuclear weapons.

Indeed, the immediate question is, why didn't President Obama strike ISIS a fatal blow when they invaded Iraq from Syria instead of dithering with failed diplomacy and failed negotiations with defunct regimes and terrorists, at the expense of our national security?

Surely, the final foreign policy failure will be to surrender Afghanistan to the Taliban -- which is inevitable and should happen sooner, not later with more losses of life and treasure -- and reassign the withdrawing troops to secure our neglected southern border.

Sadly, the president's mission creep has been extended domestic scandals and crimes against the people such as "Fast and Furious," Benghazi, the IRS, the VA hospitals, and the executive overreach of the EPA and finance enforcement.

Washington Post
June 8, 2014

Dangerously naïve Obama administration

President Obama and his minion administration are starkly naïve to think that America can make peace with the Taliban when they are now part of al-Qaida dedicated to converting everyone in the world to Islam or face death. Indeed, we cannot negotiate with Islamic terrorists any more than negotiating with Iran to keep them from creating nuclear weapons to destroy Israel and make war with the West.

New York Times
May 14, 2014

President Obama aims for repeat of housing crash

President Obama, newly appointed Fannie-Freddie regulator Mel Watt, HUD Secretary Donovan, Treasury Secretary Lew, Federal Reserve Chairwoman, Yellen and the Dodd-Frank Finance laws are in the process of creating a repeat of the 2007/2008 housing and finance crash -- created by President Clinton, HUD director Andrew Cuomo and Attorney General Janet Reno's forced lowering of home lending standards for unqualified buyers in their insane drive for affordable housing -- indeed, with the abuse of power using President Carter's foolish Community Reinvestment Act.

Clearly, President Obama's move to repeat the Clinton disaster to recover the foundering housing market is surely the insanity of repeating the cause of the collapse hoping for a different result. Instead, Obama's blind ambition for his legacy will surely result in hastening the reality of the looming economic bubble to burst prematurely, causing tidal waves of economic misery and pain. Alas, President Obama's flagrant abuses of executive power is certainly on track to "fundamentally transform" the social, political and economic core of America into a runaway train wreck causing the demise of liberty, prosperity and our republic of freedom.

Our only hope is for a fundamental transformation of Congress and the Presidency in the 2014 and 2016 elections.

Wall Street Journal
February 20, 2014

Re: **Medicare Advantage Democrats - editorial**

The WSJ's February 20, 2014 editorial regarding the Medicare Advantage Democrats is clearly on target. "Look who's defending George Bush's health plan for seniors"

President Bush's Medicare Advantage program was the best thing that happened to Medicare seniors since its inception. Government's failure to reduce and eliminate the vast fraud, waste and abuse in Medicare and Medicaid is bad enough. However, President Obama's early assault on Medicare Advantage -- as a presidential candidate -- plus the forced passage of Obama/Democrat Unaffordable Health Careless Act that attacks Medicare Advantage with forthcoming cuts was unconscionable.

Particularly, when 28% of seniors are enrolled in Medicare Advantage, and one of two people eligible for Medicare chooses Advantage, and enrollment is growing at a 10% annual clip -- simply because government turns control of health care over to private plans that manage Medicare, with more flexible services and benefits than traditional Medicare, and "seamless delivery of health care services," -- for better health care outcomes, and higher quality health care.

My wife and I are enrolled in Kaiser Senior Advantage, which is the leading Medicare Advantage manager and a shining example for other Advantage programs to emulate. Indeed, we received the best of care -- well worth the premiums -- and we firmly believe it should be the standard for all senior health care.

Leading Senate Democrats, who voted for Obamacare -- and are now opposing the cuts to Medicare Advantage because they are up for re-election -- are little more than pandering political hypocrites who will slice Medicare Advantage the day after their re-election. Senior voters in their states should not buy the snake oil. If they do, they will certainly pay the price of deception with less health care and higher prices.

Clearly, no time for making deals with the devils, and the devils know it. Especially, when the flow of Boomers into Medicare will substantially increase Medicare Advantage enrollment. That's the good news for seniors, and the bad news for President Obama and Democrats.

Los Angeles Times
January 17, 2014

Colby fire mismanaged

As a former lead fire dispatcher and inmate fire camp sheriff's deputy -- at Tujunga and San Gabriel Canyons -- who has followed the mismanagement of fires by the U.S. Forest Service, I can say that the Old fire, Station fire, the Colby fire in Glendora and other major fires could have been stopped while the burned acreage was small if the Forest Service had widespread contracts for Canadian Super Scoopers and DC 10 super tankers for immediate response to forest and brush fires.

Worse, it's bad enough the Forest Service mismanages U.S. Forest land by not thinning forests or clearing grounds and failing to control tree deaths from bark beetles. But when their incompetence allowing Controlled Burns -- since renamed "Prescribed Burns" -- to spread into enormous forest fires in the West, and environmental hypocrisy, causes massive air pollution like the Colby fire smoke covering the Los Angeles area, overall Forest Service policies and regulations are in dire need of reform.

Better yet, most federal lands should be turned over to the states for local control, smart privatization and economic revitalization.

Orange County Register
January 15, 2014

Ron Thomas and state abandoned his son

The tragedy of Kelly Thomas' death notwithstanding, the seriously mentally ill schizophrenic young man would not have lost his life if it were not for being abandoned by his father. Ron Thomas could have and should have had Kelly committed to a mental institution for care and rehabilitation, his safety and the safety of others.

Indeed, as a former peace officer, Ron Thomas should have known about the avenues open to him to rescue his son from the streets. Being retired from 41 years of service and experience in the criminal justice system, I know that Ron Thomas could have prevented the tragedy instead of having his son call out for his help when it was obviously too late.

Unfortunately, Ron Thomas blamed everyone but himself, and took the unconscionable position of media-driven grandstanding and gaining fame by condemning police officers doing their duty under perilous circumstances -- too often in these violent, trying times of selfish interests and extremes.

Alas, two things are certain: Ron Thomas should not profit from his own irresponsibility. And much of the irresponsibility here must be heaped on the State of California for its grave failure to meet the dire needs of the mentally ill.

Los Angeles Times
December 13, 2013

Re: **332,000 people added to state**

Acceptable illegal immigration has ruined California

Immigration has increased and most of the 332,000 population increase -- to California's now 38.2 million people -- was due to births, most of which are illegal immigration anchor babies, which continues our state's road to ruin from unconscionable, reckless liberal policies.

California's extreme liberal/progressive ideology has invited well over 2 million illegal immigrants to the state costing citizen taxpayers $billions annually for education, welfare, healthcare and crime.

Indeed, California is the perfect example of why anchor babies -- for the sole purpose of citizenship to allow mothers/parents to remain in our country -- should not be granted citizenship.

Worse, our state government has been controlled by liberal Democrats -- now a supermajority in the Legislature -- who are responsible for the insidious social, political and economic condition of California with over-regulation and punishing taxation to increase their power.

Even worse, illegal immigrants are responsible for enormous increases in gangs, murders, and other violent crime, thefts and burglaries -- and the overcrowding of our prisons -- which is causing federal courts, AB 109 and Governor Brown to release violent criminals to prey upon us indiscriminately.

Californians need to take a stand to make it all stop or continue to suffer the ongoing and increased consequences.

Los Angeles Times
November 23, 2013

Re: **New breed in the Senate**

Obama's Senate power grab

Democrat Senate majority leader Harry Reid, the new breed in the Senate and other Obama lemmings removed the filibuster and 60 vote majority for federal court nominees and other executive appointments in a power grab that will allow President Obama to stack the federal courts with liberal activist judges to protect ObamaCare and carry out Obama's bidding for the remainder of his second term. That's simply a dictatorial abuse of power, unconscionable and un-American.

USA TODAY
November 22, 2013

Re: **How well is health care working?**

President Obama's promise to extend cancelled insurance policies for a year was rejected by "Covered California," which leaves one million Californians without health insurance. That is one million out of five million health insurance policies canceled nationwide. Under ObamaCare chaos, that number is expected to swell to between 50 and 100 million as the "Unaffordable Careless Act" continues to steamroll over health care in America.

Wall Street Journal
November 21, 2013

Re: **ObamaCare forced Mom into Medicaid** by Nicole L. Hopkins

Nicole Hopkins' mother is one of the millions who had their health insurance cancelled or increased to unaffordable premiums as the result of ObamaCare. With few people signing up for Obamacare on government exchange web sites, a few more on state exchange sites, and many more unable to complete the process or being forced into Medicaid, it clearly demonstrates that government is incompetent -- and leads the American people to the inescapable conclusion that President Obama lied, and that the Obamacare law should be renamed, "The Unaffordable Careless Act" -- a tyranny which will ultimately and unnecessarily cost taxpayers an extra $1.2 trillion.

President Obama's press conference was essentially the same old blah, blah, blah Obama diversions. What he really meant was that people's health plans that were cancelled will be allowed to keep them for a year -- until after the 2014 elections -- hopefully to prevent losing the Senate. Of course the solidly socialist state of California won't go along with the extension, which "Covered California" just turned down even though 1 million people, and counting, have lost their health insurance.

Adding insult to injury, the Obamacare rollout is circumventing the Supreme Court's order preventing the forced expansion of Medicaid on the states, by causing people sign up for Medicaid instead of using the failed insurance exchanges, which will exacerbate the already crowded emergency rooms by Medicaid patients seeking non-emergency health care, endangering patients with real emergencies. That's unconscionable, and will increase the financial burden on the states.

New York Times
November 6, 2013

Wrong election choices in Virginia and New York

The elections of Terry McAuliffe as governor of Virginia and Bill de Blasio as mayor or New York are troubling indications of too much liberal Democrat voter indoctrination in the face of President Obama selling-out America to national health care and hardcore socialism.

If Virginia voters are foolish enough to elect a Clinton political crook as their governor, and New Yorkers blindly elect a socialist as mayor of the financial and business capitol of the world, national voters are in danger of committing social, political and economic suicide.

Indeed, if voters don't wise-up and throw enough Democrats out of Congress in 2014, and elect a Republican president instead of Obama-driven Hillary Clinton in 2016, America will be sliding down the road to serfdom without brakes.

Fortunately, there are presidential bright spots on the horizon with Chris Christie's landslide re-election as governor of New Jersey -- along with Republican Senators Rubio, Lee, Cruz -- and of course, former VP candidate Rep. Paul Ryan.

Remember, the right to vote is the power to save or let die -- as in electing Republican Assemblyman Tim Donnelly or re-electing Jerry Brown as governor of California.

USA TODAY
November 5, 2013

Obama compounded his lie about the ACA

While speaking to the America Medical Association in 2009, President Obama promised -- and repeated many times in other speeches -- "If you like your health care plan, you'll be able to keep your health care plan, period." Now, since people are angered by having their health care insurance cancelled because it didn't meet

Affordable Care Act standards, Obama changed his act. On November 4, 2013, President Obama said "If you have or had one of these plans before the Affordable Care Act came into law and you really like that plan, what WE said was you could keep it if it hasn't changed since the law was passed."

What does President Obama mean, "WE said…." when it was HE who said no such thing? Which means he seriously deceived the people into thinking they could keep their health care plans. In other words, he lied to get the law passed and has now compounded that lie. Indeed, President Obama clearly knew what was in the law when it was rammed through the Democrat Congress and he signed it.

When the Supreme Court wrongly found Obamacare constitutional because the penalty for not getting health insurance was a tax -- which was really a progressive penalty, not a tax -- the Court rightly found that forcing more Medicaid on the states for the uninsured was unconstitutional. Now people are flocking to free state Medicaid instead of signing up for Obamacare -- and Obama is telling people to do that -- which is unconstitutional.

Adding insult to injury, people were previously unable to buy health insurance across state lines, stifling competition. Now, with the ACA, people are prohibited from buying health insurance across county lines.

Certainly, Obamacare is an unconstitutional, unconscionable act that will adversely affect the economy and people's lives.

Sacramento Bee
August 24, 2013

Rim Fire next to Yosemite could have been stopped

As with so many runaway fires in the West, and now the enormous Rim Fire threatening Yosemite, if the Forest Service and Cal Fire had properly prepared for the all-too-frequent explosive fires, they would have been stopped in their tracks.

Indeed, if increased numbers and immediate use of DC-10 super air tankers had been made, high density fuel fires could have been extinguished by massive the water drops, backed-up by Canadian Super-Scoopers. All they have to do is buy or lease and deploy more of them.

Of course, most forest fires have been exacerbated by extreme and unreasonable environmental/conservationist forces, the refusal to thin forests and to combat the death of trees from bark beetles -- both of which accelerate forest fires.

Surely the time has come to either continue the unnecessary restrictions, high cost, air pollution and the unconscionable loss of life, property, forest land and watershed -- or to get smart, be prepared, and stop it.

Wall Street journal
August 18, 2013

Re: Put a corn cob in your tank - editorial

The WSJ editorial is correct, but could have been less corny and more assertive about senseless, obsolete need for the increased ethanol mandate. Indeed, corn ethanol fuel has become another poster idea for the costly failures of government's good intentions.

Surely, it's bad enough that corn ethanol is not only unnecessary for our vehicles that are becoming more fuel efficient, that increased domestic oil and gas production makes ethanol mandates even more costly and unnecessary, and that corn ethanol is robbing our corn supply -- raising the cost of our food.

It is simply unconscionable for Congress not to admit the mistake and repeal all corn ethanol additive mandates. Particularly, when ethanol ruins the engines in our vehicles, and is even more toxic than gasoline emissions. But that's politics and big government, isn't it. Pass bad laws, invoke punishing taxes and regulations, and let it ride.

Alas, that's why government growth, spending and debt are consuming our freedoms and our future. If we are to survive, voters must reign in and reverse the insanity.

New York Times
August 10, 2013

Breaking America's economic back

Illegally exempting unions and congressional staff from Obamacare, along with pushing the implementation until after the 2014 elections comes as no surprise.

Particularly when President Obama continues to circumvent the law with EPA and Energy executive orders and edicts destined to hurt the middle class.

Lest we forget, the president's Obamacareless monster was created by then Senator Obama while running in the 2008 election. He created a crisis that didn't exist. Of course the crisis that did exist, and persists, is the Clinton/Frank/Dodd Democrat-caused housing and financial crash.

Healthcare in America needed some work, but not with national health care that will surely break our economic back. The Democrat Congress that rammed it through without debate, shares the blame. Indeed, every House and Senate member who voted for it.

Washington Post
August 7, 2013

Losing the war on terror

The Obama administration's national security malfeasance and the Army are at fault for their failure to discover, identify and prosecute Major Hasan as an enemy combatant terrorist. The Fort Hood shootings were planned acts of terror and the assassination of our troops, not "work place violence." Major Hasan should be convicted of terrorism, treason, stripped of his citizenship and executed.

Los Angeles Times
July 29, 2013

NBC miniseries "Hillary" set for 2016 presidential elections

The forthcoming NBC miniseries "Hillary" -- set to premiere just before the 2016 presidential elections -- removes all doubt that NBC and the rest of the liberal news media are not only in the tank for the Democratic Party, they are actively campaigning for the Democrat agenda. Indeed, what could be more historical than electing the first woman president after the election of the first African-American president?

Of course NBC has a long, active record of promoting the liberal agenda as evidenced by Aaron Sorkin's "West Wing," as a fantasy 1999 to 2006 Democrat presidency television series paralleling the Republican presidency of George Bush. Sorkin's characters and clever dialogue seduced the viewing audience into making "West Wing" a major success.

However, Sorkin wasn't finished promoting his insidious liberal agenda with his new HBO series, "Newsroom," which is a utopian story about cable news network, "Atlantis Cable News." The problem is, Sorkin's clever characters and dialogue doesn't mask the hideous story line of a so-called moderate Republican news anchor equating "The Tea Party with the Taliban," and demonizing the Republican candidates with personal attacks in the 2012 presidential election with the second season.

Free speech is one thing, but radical liberal television networks, writers and producers dealing with politics, government and ideology should not be immune from insidious slander and defamation against conservatives or anyone. After all, America is not exclusive to big government and the liberal elite. Regular, free people have owned this country from its constitutional inception. And it's time to foreclose on the tyranny of self-serving squatters.

Washington Times
July 27, 2013

Phony scandals? - No - Phony president

President Obama's perpetual campaign continues with the latest round of biased media-supported, staged travel-trivia speeches -- stroking the economy and the middle class -- with his clueless people backdrops of bobble heads nodding and applauding his every point, on queue.

Of course, Obama's latest charges against his Republican opponents -- of causing Washington to take its eye off the ball with "distractions, political posturing and phony scandals" -- are in fact his phony-in-chief maneuvers to detract from his abusive government, social, political, economic and national security failures.

Meanwhile, the president relentlessly continues his unprecedented abuse of power, executive orders and edicts, political appointments, and administrative regulations forcing his destructive injustice, miseducation, energy, environmental, healthcare, immigration, financial, debt and spending agenda upon America.

Los Angeles Times
July 20, 2013

Re: **A president reflects on race**

The most divisive president

President Obama's Trayvon Martin-driven remarks regarding race do little to nothing to relieve tensions brought on by the intense radical African-American leaders' reaction to George Zimmerman's "Not Guilty" verdict that resulted in a national call to protest the perceived injustice of justice being served in the Florida court. Indeed, the president failed to recognize or condemn the violence, and did nothing to dispel the self-inflicted stereotype.

In fact, President Obama's divisive racial statements exacerbated the resulting violence and rioting in the streets of Los Angeles and elsewhere with gangs of African-American juveniles and young adults assaulting and robbing innocent people, looting stores and setting fires -- including two American flags. Indeed, now there is another media-driven Al Sharpton-Jesse Jackson move to protest in 100 major cities across America.

Alas, lest we forget, the Trayvon Martin/George Zimmerman conflict was not black and white. It was black and Hispanic.

Clearly, America has been placed in deepening social, political and economic stress, chaos and deterioration by the most divisive president in our history. One who's blind social justice political agenda -- supported by congressional Democrats -- has grown government with a tyrannical war against free market Capitalism, imposing economy-crushing national health care, costly green energy, spending, insurmountable debt, abused his personal power and abdicated our national security.

USA TODAY
July 15, 2013

Re: Zimmerman verdict taps into a deep vein of distrust - editorial

I strongly disagree with USA TODAY'S notion that "Trayvon Martin's death remains an avoidable American tragedy -- one that Zimmerman set into motion.

Indeed, George Zimmerman's life has been destroyed by a permanent unjust media-driven racial lynching promoted by the exploitive racism of people like Jesse Jackson and Al Sharpton, exacerbated by African-American activists and President Obama. If it were not for the obsessive media, national hostile demonstrations, rioting and closing a major freeway in California would not be going on and continuing.

Alas, as long as the Jacksons, Sharptons and others continue to exploit one-sided racism for power and profit, there will be no racial harmony.

Surely, the ultimate injustice would be Holder's Justice Department persecuting Zimmerman with a civil rights charge, which should not be done because Zimmerman was not acting "under color of authority."

Washington Post
July 4, 2013

Declare independence from big government

Sadly, as we celebrate the 4th of July Independence Day of our founding, we are faced with a government that has become as tyrannical and intrusive as the government from which we separated. Our hard won freedoms are being lost to big government dependency, unreasonable taxation, punishing regulations and too much government growth, spending, debt, and control of property, education, health care, and the free market.

Unfortunately, the time has come to declare our independence again by reinforcing the founding intent of our Constitution, reducing government to its basic responsibilities of our unique republic, our Congress, Executive, judiciary, national defense, treasury, interstate commerce and foreign policy. Taxation must be reformed to become either a fair flat tax, consumption tax or a combination thereof. And we must have an unfettered free market.

Indeed, state sovereignty and government by consent of the governed must be renewed or we will never be truly free.

Wall Street Journal
July 3, 2013

Re: Health law penalties delayed

Obamacare's fatal flaw was inherent in the scheme

Obamacare penalties for employers of over 50 employees forced to provide health insurance being delayed until after the 2014 mid-term elections is simply another political ploy to delay the impact of Obamacare's abuse of power, just as President Obama avoided re-election defeat in the 2012 presidential elections by delaying, distracting and lying to the electorate.

Worse, the Obama administration is implementing a program indoctrinating students to convince their parents to support Obamacare, which furthers Obama's master plan to fundamentally transform America from a democratic republic to European-style socialism with national healthcare.

Even worse, President Obama is not only plunging Americans into $2 trillion of additional healthcare debt -- when all that was needed was deep Medicare and Medicaid reform -- his insidious green energy and automotive fuel standards will make electricity and fuel costs "Necessarily skyrocket" for our own good.

All of which -- coupled with selling-out our education, economy and national security at every level -- will leave America in ruins.

USA TODAY
June 28, 2013

Re: It's a sad day for democracy - by Brian S. Brown.

I agree. Voters lose, gay federal judge and tyranny of the minority win

The Chief Justice Roberts and the Supreme Court majority betrayed democracy and the Constitution by saying the sponsors of Proposition 8 did not have legal standing to appeal after the ballot measure was struck down by Vaughn Walker, a gay a federal judge in San Francisco. Both decisions against the majority of California voters were unconstitutional and unconscionable.

It didn't matter that former Attorney General, now Governor Jerry Brown and Attorney General Kamala Harris violated their oaths of office by refusing to defend Proposition 8 simply because they were against the will of the people, who passed the state constitutional amendment by a 52 percent vote, prohibiting gay marriage.

Alas, the tyranny of San Francisco and the gay minority by social intimidation and legal extortion have dealt fatal blows to our legal system and the traditional institution of marriage, confirming the dangers of what is becoming a superficial society of moral decay, social aggression, political terrorism, selfish interests and extremes.

Los Angeles Times
June 27, 2013

Re: Gay marriages should start now: AG Kamala Harris

California Attorney General Kamala Harris doesn't want the 9th Circuit Court of Appeals wait the usual 25 days to lift its Prop. 8 stay, and start gay marriages NOW!

It doesn't matter that former Attorney General, now Governor Jerry Brown and Attorney General Kamala Harris violated their oaths of office by refusing to defend Proposition 8 simply because they were against the will of the people, who passed the state constitutional amendment by a 52 percent vote, prohibiting gay marriage.

Indeed, overturning Proposition 8 comes from the tyranny of the minority, which rules California and most of the United States. Gay extremists and activist courts have joined environmental extremists in a long record of intimidating anyone or anything that opposes them.

Likewise, the 1994 voter referendum, Proposition 187, passed by 59 percent of the vote, prohibiting illegal aliens from using health care, education, welfare and other social services -- which were costing California taxpayers $3 billion per year -- was ruled unconstitutional by an activist federal court, which stood because Governor Gray Davis violated his oath of office, halted state appeals and refused to defend the law.

Of course, the tyranny of the minority has been perpetuated by liberal Democrats' insidious agenda of lies and deceit, punishing laws, taxes and regulations wagging the public dog from the Sacramento state house -- steadily driving California toward social, political and economic ruin.

Alas, California liberals -- the worst in the nation -- have rejected traditional American values and created a superficial society of moral decay, social aggression, political terrorism, selfish interests and extremes.

USA TODAY
June 25, 2013

President Obama ignores China/Russia rejection to return Snowden

Instead of dealing directly with the rejections by China and Russia to the return of criminally-charged NSA leaker/fugitive/traitor, Edward Snowden, President Obama has chosen to ignore the national security crisis -- along with the Benghazi and IRS scandals -- and deflect attention away from his domestic and international failures by assisting Syrian rebels, reducing our nuclear power deterrent, and campaigning against global warming.

Indeed, President Obama is adding insult to injury by limiting oil exploration and production, pushing expensive green fuel, wind and solar energy, carbon taxing coal energy, industrial and business emissions, and implementing unnecessary/economy-crushing Obamacare. Clearly, with Obama and company in charge, there has been little or no direct leadership in dealing with real social, political, economic, and increasing national security threats.

Alas, Mr. Obama appears to be a presidential imposter who only knows the deceit of distraction, perpetual campaigning and manufactured crisis, with no accountability.

Sacramento Bee
June 21, 2013

Federal courts abuse power against California

Governor Brown's dispute with the federal court over the release of state prison inmates goes far beyond compliance by prison re-alignment, which has already impacted local county jails and endangered communities. Now, the three-judge 'Star Chamber' has order the immediate release of 9,600 state prisoners, which will put California citizens in eminent danger. However, liberal California government bears a substantial part of the blame for crowded prison conditions.

Indeed, state and federal Democrats are responsible for tyrannical government growth and the proliferation of illegal aliens, by failure to enforce immigration laws, inviting illegals to partake in welfare, education and healthcare, particularly in California, which is costing California taxpayers about $5 billion per year. Plus overloading our prisons with illegal alien criminals to a point where the federal court ordered nearly 10,000 prisoners released early to prey on California citizens.

Wise-up, California voters, and put a stop to the political insanity. Our security, our economy, our future and the future of our children are at stake.

New York Times
June 20, 2013

Obama's national insecurity

President Obama's track record on national security has been a dangerous policy backing off. And clearly, the terrorists and our other enemies know it, as evidenced by Obama's support of American-style liberal democracy in the revolutionary "Arab Spring," which was obviously compromised by Islamic extremists, consuming North Africa and the Middle East, including our vital ally, Turkey.

Indeed, al-Qaeda and the Muslim Brotherhood are alive and well, in a constant state of growth and power. Plus, regardless of our losses, Obama has ensured that Iraq and Afghanistan will certainly come back to bite America, when Iraq is taken over by Iran, and Afghanistan is returned to the al-Qaeda-friendly Taliban.

Coupled with President Obama's unilateral reduction of our nuclear deterrent power, while failing to deter China, North Korea, Russia, Pakistan and Iran from nuclear proliferation -- and failing to secure our borders -- his lack of national security performance is unconscionable.

Surely, with President Obama at the helm, helping Syrian rebels is just another exercise in futility, while we are in a deepening state of national insecurity.

Los Angles Times
June 18, 2013

California's Democrat-voter-and-fed-assisted economic suicide

California's AB-32 cap-and-tax revenues - which are supposed to fund green energy programs -- will be diverted by Gov. Brown and the Democrat Legislature to increase Welfare and Medicaid funding by $500 million this year, and the diversions will increase to between $ 2 billion and $15 billion by 2015.

It doesn't seem to matter that the Democrat legislature's recently passed $96.3 billion state budget does nothing to address California's enormous debt. Or that embracing the fraud of Obamacare will raise insurance rates for all Californians, increase the cost of living and decrease employment.

Adding insult to injury, and new federal mandates for increased ethanol in gasoline will raise gas prices, destroy auto and diesel engines, and increase air pollution with insidious toxins. Plus, the increase of corn-ethanol will raise food prices significantly.

Sadly, with Democrat-voter-and-fed-assisted economic suicide in the works, California will surely go into a long political tailspin, nose-dive and crash.

The Wall Street Journal
June 15, 2013

RE: Dabbling in Syria - editorial

As the WSJ editorial aptly put it, President Obama is indeed "Dabbling in Syria." And he is losing the war against terrorism.

President Obama's decision to provide arms and support to Syrian rebels is simply a distraction from administration scandals -- in the IRS, Dept. of Justice, and Dept. of State -- and will certainly be an exercise in futility.

Particularly, in light of Iran and Russia's support of the Syrian regime, and Obama's rebel support of regime turnovers in Egypt,

Libya and throughout North Africa and the Middle East, giving al-Qaeda, the Muslim Brotherhood and other Islamic militants blanket power.

Indeed, the terrorist threats to our national security have substantially increased, benchmarked by the malfeasance in Benghazi costing the lives of our ambassador and three other Americans.

Surely, history has taught us that it's better to deal with dictatorship regimes we know, than the world-domination Islamists who won't.

Los Angeles Times
May 27, 2013

Re: Fracking: How Risky? – editorial

Re: Brown prison policy repeal sought

California calamity
It comes as no surprise that the Los Angeles Times and others are suggesting delays in fracking 15 billion barrels of oil from the Central Valley's 1,750 square mile Monterey Shale formation between Modesto and Bakersfield, which goes along with extreme environmentalists intentions to always file lawsuits against additional oil and natural gas production from California's ample resources. Indeed, it doesn't seem to matter that fracking has proven to be safe, or that it would create tens of thousands of jobs and reduce California gas prices.

Surely, Californians will increasingly suffer from the calamity being brought on from unreasonable environmentalists and conservationists who have decreased water supplies from the Sacramento Delta to Central Valley farms, Southern California populations, and raised the cost of living with tyrannical regulations.

Indeed, coupled with the enormous cost of the teachers' unions and California miseducation, the open door policy for illegal immigrants to suck our public welfare, education and health care dry, Governor Brown's prison re-alignment policy endangering the lives of the people, AB 32's negative impact on our economy, and the corrosive Democrat cartel's control of government in Sacramento, the outlook for California's survival is bleak at best.

Certainly worse, from voter-assisted economic suicide, the high speed rail boondoggle, and runway debt.

The Washington Post
May 25, 2013

President Obama's chilling effect

From the time presidential candidate Barack Obama campaigned on fundamentally transforming America, his presidential actions, diversions, distractions and deceptions tantamount to outright lies paved the way to accomplishing his liberal agenda -- beginning with ramming his national health care legislation through a complicit Democrat Congress.

Indeed, from then on it was steady government and regulatory growth, spending and insurmountable debt by leaps and bounds -- all supported by the liberal state media, who got President Obama elected and led him into a second term, but not before he lost the House of Representatives to Republicans backed by the spontaneously formed Tea Party in opposition to the president's health care-less laws, spending and insurmountable debt.

No thanks to the liberal press and years of liberal indoctrination of students by the education establishment, most of America is clueless about President Obama and his administration's insidious machinations undermining the Constitution, and the deep freeze chilling effect he has on his opposition -- as evidenced by the IRS targeting the Tea Party, conservative groups and individuals -- and the Justice Department targeting Associated Press and Fox News reporters.

Of course, as usual, President Obama feigned outrage at the exposures, fired the IRS Commissioner, and ordered his Attorney General Eric Holder to review policies and investigate, even though Holder had signed the order to investigate FOX's Chief Washington Correspondent, James Rosen as a co-conspirator on a national security leak. Surely, Holder investigating "Fast and Furious" Holder and his blatant abuse of power is a redundant gesture.

Alas, lest we forget, it is President Obama's dictatorial regulations, legislative tyrannies, government growth and his gang of liberal Democrats that are limiting our free speech and liberties -- ruining our economy and our culture, not to mention risking our national security by toying with terrorism -- when it is much smaller limited constitutional government that we need to survive.

Wall Street Journal
May 17, 2013

Re: The IRS scandal started at the top

Re: Nina Olson for IRS Commissioner

President Obama responsible for IRS targets

It's becoming painfully clear that President Obama's fingerprints are all over the IRS tyrannies against the Tea Party, conservative groups and individuals. Indeed, the president's demonization of the Tea Party and conservative groups set the tone for his IRS and captains of political corruption to target and silence them.

In early 2010, President Obama gave marching orders to Democrat activists to attack Tea Party and conservative groups, and for congressional Democrats to pressure the IRS to target them. Of course, the SEIU attacked and Democrat Senators, Chuck Shumer, Al Franken and others complied by pushing the IRS to take action.

Certainly, the 2012 presidential election put the IRS targeting in high gear against Obama's opponent, Mitt Romney's supporters, including wealthy Idaho businessman and long time Republican supporter and donor, Frank VanderSloot, who was demonized and audited three times in four months.

President Obama's IRS hatchet man, acting Commissioner, Steve Miller contemptuously testified before a congressional House Committee, side-stepping questions and confirming nothing but feigned ignorance and Sarah Hall Ingram's position as executive in charge of the tax-exempt division, which in 2010 began targeting the Tea Party, conservative groups, evangelical and pro-Israel groups.

Unfortunately, Ingram -- who received unconscionable bonuses for her dirty work -- was recently promoted to serve as director of the IRS Obamacare program office, which will rain down tax tyrannies forcing compliance with Mr. Obama's ideological crown jewel, which will further damage or reverse economic recovery.

Surely, vast tax reform is needed, which should begin with the appointment of IRS National Taxpayer Advocate Nina Olson -- the ombudsman for the public inside the IRS -- as IRS Commissioner, instead of President Obama's inside man, Daniel Werfel, current White House Budget Office manager.

WSJ editorial recommending Olson is correct. Alas, the problem could be resolved entirely by the passage of the Fair (consumption) Tax, which would eliminate the IRS.

Los Angeles Times
May 16, 2013

Fire services fail in use of DC 10 air tankers

10 Tanker Air Carrier moving its two DC 10 fire fighting tankers from the Southern California Logistics Airport in Victorville to Wyoming -- to suit its new federal contract -- would be a great loss to Southern California fire suppression, if the tankers had been used by Cal Fire and the U.S. Forest Service properly.

Surely, if the DC 10 tankers had been used to make their massive water drops when the enormous Camarillo fire and the current Frasier Park fire first started, the fires would have been extinguished -- end of story. Indeed, if they were used on the Oak Hills fire before it crested the Southwest area of the Cajon Pass, the fire would not have spread any further.

Certainly, the U.S. Forest Service has a dismal record in fire fighting throughout the country, and certainly in California. If they had called in the DC 10 tankers on the fire that devastated the San

Bernardino National Forest Lake Arrowhead area, and the Station Fire in the Angeles National Forest, the losses would have been minimal.

Clearly, if state and national fire services used DC 10 air tankers and Canadian Super Scoopers the way they should -- instead of going on the cheap -- the overall cost of wildfires would be greatly reduced. Many calls for local fire personnel and equipment to assist, would be unnecessary, and it not take away from their local availability to the people they serve.

Public service nonfeasance, needlessly costing lives and property is simply unconscionable.

Wall Street Journal
May 13, 2013

Re: GOP demands apology - front page

Re: Benghazi hearings

President Obama's mounting articles of impeachment

It's already obvious that the 9/11 anniversary Benghazi, Libya terrorist attack costing the lives of our ambassador and three security personnel was the result of intentional malfeasance by President Obama and Secretary of State Clinton.

Worse, the deceitful cover-up is tantamount to giving aid and comfort to our Islamic jihadist terrorist enemy to further a re-election campaign and to protect Obama and Clinton at any cost.

Even worse, the ongoing Teflon provided by the ideology-driven liberal media to President Obama and presumptive 2016 nominee Hillary Clinton -- and the demonization of all opposition -- is an unconscionable abdication of public responsibility by the press.

It was bad enough that the President Obama's campaign promises supporting the passage of Obamacare were a pack of lies concealing the devastating costs and cuts in America's healthcare coverage -- in addition to the wasteful, useless spending of his enormous stimulus packages, economy-busting regulations, national debt expansion.

Now comes reports that as early as the 2010 passage of Obamacare, and during the re-election campaign, administrative tyranny was launched by President Obama's IRS against the Tea Party and other conservative opposition's tax exemption status -- in addition to the merciless demonizing of all opposition of any description. Indeed, even the New York Times criticized the administration's abusive IRS tactics against the Tea Party in a March 2012 editorial.

Subsequently, the president's sequester idea developed into selective pain from government cuts in FAA air traffic controllers and all manner of other unnecessary cuts designed to adversely affect the public -- placing blame on Republicans -- all intended to reclaim Democrat control of the House of Representatives in 2014.

Certainly, President Obama has made it painfully and abundantly clear that he has no problem defying Congress, ignoring the constraints of the Constitution, and the will of the people to do or get what he wants -- un-American as it may be.

Clearly, President Obama's costly ideology-driven executive orders, and administrative edicts and regulations amounting to tyrannical administrative abuse of power and cover-ups, along with patterns of lies and deceit, dereliction of duty against terrorism, border security -- and his failings in national and domestic security -- are stacking up as prospective articles of impeachment.

Lest we forget, it was House Republicans who moved ahead with hearings on the Watergate cover-up and articles of impeachment against former Republican president Nixon's abuse of power resulting in his resignation. Which begs the question: Where are the Democrats in the mounting evidence against President Obama and his captains of corruption?.

The problem is: President Obama will likely never be impeached and convicted because congressional Democrats and the liberal press are unlikely to let it happen -- and America will undoubtedly suffer the consequences.

Wall Street Journal
April 26, 2013

Obama administration endangers our security

President Obama and his Attorney General Holder are making it painfully clear that they have no problem risking our national security by cutting off the FBI questioning of Boston bomber, Dzhokhar Trarnaev with a U.S Attorney, a federal magistrate, and an appointed federal defense attorney advising the terrorist of his Miranda rights -- which he immediately exercised.

Worse, it doesn't seem to matter that Dzhokhar is a radical Islamic jihadist traitor waging war against America -- who along with his deceased brother Tamerian -- planned to bomb Time Square in New York, or that what the Obama administration did, increased threats to our national and domestic security.

In other words, President Obama, AG Eric Holder, his U.S. Attorney, and the federal magistrate blatantly abdicated their sworn duty to defend our public safety against all enemies, foreign and domestic, leaving them with the blood of Boston on their hands. That, along with failures against Islamic Fort Hood and Benghazi terrorism amounts to unconscionable aid and comfort to our enemies -- tantamount to impeachable treason.

Sacramento Bee
April 18, 2013

Governor Brown and the Sacramento Democrat cartel

Governor Brown's deceit in selling-out voters with the Proposition 30 tax-con and high speed rail boondoggle can only be eclipsed by the Democrat supermajority cartel in the Legislature -- poised to dilute Proposition 13, the voter-initiative process, pass destructive laws and raise taxes.

For too long, California Democrats have set the good and bad examples for other states with good voter-initiatives and Proposition 13's tax restraints, and the bad open-door policies for welfare recipients and illegal aliens to feed upon housing, education and health care benefits, costing taxpayers $5 billion per year.

Coupled with enormous corporate and personal taxation to support growing government, the powerful teachers' union, the miseducation of our students -- AB 32 and the global warming environmental costs, and the steady flow of regulations raising the cost of living -- there is no doubt that California's economy is crashing from business flight and unemployment.

Adding injury to the intimidation of the state's failed criminal justice system, AB 109's prison re-alignment is dumping felony inmates on county jails to serve their time, causing early releases of dangerous criminals and aliens, who threaten our business, neighborhoods and our personal safety.

Question is: how long will it take for naÃ¯ve voters to suffer enough pain to realize they have been taken for a fool's ride, and that dumping legislation-crazed Democrats is the only solution for California's recovery. Surely, the same goes for our federal government and the recovery of America.

Los Angeles Times
April 14, 2013

President Obama: Political poison ivy

President Obama's socialist agenda-driven performance during his first term and three months into his second term is clear and convincing evidence that he is not only a dictatorial zealot -- recklessly pushing national health care, costly green energy and environmental regulations, self-destructive spending, negative economic policy, and unsustainable debt -- he is an incompetent-in-chief with his failures in foreign policy, terrorism, and our national and domestic security.

Surely, the Obama administration is not taking Putin's Russian gangster and anti-American activities seriously, or their blatant support for terrorist regimes, or their energy deals with China increasing the economic threat to America. Coupled with continually diminishing our constitutional rights, protections and freedoms -- make the president an ambivalent danger to our country and our people.

President Obama's sellout to the UN, and his casual lack of purpose -- when confronted by al-Qaeda forces in North Africa and the Middle-East, Iran's nuclear threats against Israel and America, and his gross failures in Libya and Egypt -- is simply unconscionable. Worse, the immediate nuclear threats from North Korea's insane leader against South Korea, Japan and America highlights our inexcusable lack of ICBM defense, is cause for deep concerns.

One thing is certain. The Spring cherry blossom event in Washington cannot conceal the political poison Ivy creeping from the White House to the Capitol, throughout government and the nation -- stinging America wherever it hurts the most. Indeed, reversals of Democrat-driven damage may not come soon enough in 2014 and 2016.

Washington Post
April 11, 2013

President has no budget plan

President Obama's budget plan, along with his targeted sequester, can only be described as unconscionable deceptions, intimidation and petty political extortion at the expense of the economy and the middle class.

Indeed, President Obama has no "budget" plan. Budgets require a positive outcome for income and expenditures. Instead, the president is acting like an irresponsible child with a no-limit taxpayers' credit card.

Washington Times
February 2, 2013

Re: The Gay Scouts of America - editorial
I agree wholeheartedly with the WT editorial, and call upon the Boy Scouts of America leadership to stick by our standards

Victims of pedophile Catholic priests and Boy Scout leaders have suffered years of agony while the press persecutes the church and the BSA, avoiding the real cause of what is a national disgrace. Contrary to popular politically correct belief, gays are not sacred cows.

Indeed, little to nothing has been revealed about how -- as a result of the sexual revolution in the 1970's and 1980's -- gay pedophiles flocked to Catholic seminaries to become priests because they would have a constant source of altar boys to prey upon.

Media persecution has now advanced against the Boy Scouts of America, the victim of gay pedophile assaults by scout leaders from the same period and beyond, seriously damaging the best character-building program in America and the world for boys and young men.

Worse, gay activists have a history of aggression against any opposition to them or gay marriage. However, the gay community has never condemned the insidious practices in the church and the BSA, nor have they done anything to discourage or prevent it -- yet still remain silent -- except to condemn the BSA for excluding gays.

As an active Bronze Palm Eagle Scout, district executive board member, and supporter of the BSA -- retired from 41 years in law enforcement and the criminal justice system -- I strongly encourage the BSA to stick to our standards and not give-in to PC pressure or gay intimidation. The Boy Scouts and Girl Scouts are substantial last best hopes of each new generation. To lose them would be unconscionable.

USA TODAY
January 28, 2013

60 Minutes/Obama anoint Hillary for president

After anointing Obama twice for president, 60 Minutes' fawning interview with Secretary of State, Hillary Clinton and President Obama -- arranged by the president as an obvious endorsement -- led the media's way to anointing Hillary and Bill Clinton president for 2016.

Indeed, the manner in which the dominant national media gushed over Clinton's stellar performance -- and feigned emotion -- in the congressional hearings over the mishandling of the Benghazi, Libya terrorist assassinations of four Americans was an early indicator.

Clearly, the liberal media are bound and determined to elect the first woman president following the first black president to make their place in history, even if it costs the life of America.

Los Angeles Times
January 27, 2013

Re: State 'did the impossible', Brown says - front page

California doing the impossible is an impossible dream

Governor Brown's State of the State speech projecting that, "California did the impossible" in emerging from a financial crisis is an impossible dream yet to be realized, even with Proposition 30's and AB 32's projected tax revenues.

Surely, promoting an overhaul of education funding, building the high speed rail and aggressively expanding healthcare to the needy, while ignoring the enormous voter-approved accumulated debt, illustrates economic delusion.

Indeed, when Governor Brown goes to the Governor's conference in Washington touting his California plans as a model for the nation, he will discover that President Obama has already been there, done that, and seeking more damages.

Certainly, the liberal lemmings who facilitated Governor Brown and President Obama's self-destructive transformations will painfully realize the second coming of a worse recession resulting from hard-core government malfeasance. Problem is, they're taking the rest of us down with them.

Wall Street Journal
January 26, 2013

Re: SEC nominee signals shift

Obama's personal SEC cop

Considering President Obama's record of nominees and particularly questionable appointments, it seems quite evident that his nomination of tough former U.S. Attorney, Mary Jo White to head the SEC, is another move to deepen the expansion of his personal power on Wall Street and American business.

Particularly when White would be the first prosecutor to run the SEC, along with her extensive connections in representing major banking players such as J.P. Morgan Chase, Morgan Stanley, and defending Bank of America's former CEO, Ken Lewis against securities fraud.

Needles to say, it's disturbing for the enforcement of bad new finance laws, and deeply troubling for our economy and future.